HELL
IS SO GREEN

HELL
IS SO GREEN

Search and Rescue over the Hump in World War II

Lt. William Diebold

Edited with a foreword and afterword by
Richard Matthews

LYONS PRESS
Guilford, Connecticut
An imprint of Globe Pequot Press

To the men and women who have served in wars,
and those who had an extraordinary capacity
for saving the lives of others

FOREWORD

Lt. William Diebold, who served in the Army's Air Transport Command (ATC) in the China-Burma-India (CBI) theater during World War II, never fired a weapon in battle. Like many of the men in the ATC, soldiers and airmen who flew supplies over the Hump, he never saw combat—at least not the kind where men shoot at each other with the intent to kill or destroy. But Diebold fought the Japanese in Burma and China as effectively as any infantryman or fighter pilot. He did it by saving lives.

What follows is an extraordinary, largely untold story. Books have been written about the Hump, certainly, but most of those accounts focus on the flyers, the men who crossed the highest mountains of the world through some of the world's worst weather almost daily to keep the Allied armies in China supplied with fuel, food, and weapons against imperial Japan. Some of those pilots and crewmen went down over the jungles of northern Burma and Tibet, dying as their planes, flying in zero visibility, slammed into the sides of mountains. Heavy icing caused engines to fail, and Japanese Zeros attacked often as well. Some bailed out, but even then many perished in the impenetrable and unforgiving country they parachuted into.

Of the nearly three thousand men who went down over the Hump between 1943 and 1945, some twelve hundred made it back to safety. Some of them made it back because of Diebold.

Pilot Don Downie survived eighty-two missions flying over the Himalayas into China. The author of *Flying the Hump*, he had this to say about Lieutenant Diebold:

> *Bill had more guts than any man I've ever met. When sober, he bails out of Army planes into the green hell of the Burma jungle in search of lost pilots and other flight crews. When on a binge, he revels in chopping the legs off beds, decapitating mosquito nets with a machete, shooting out lights with a carbine, and firing signal flares through the length of our grass-topped basha. [But] aside from my parachute, I felt he was the best life insurance I had when I flew the Burma Hump.*

If that sounds a little like the antics of a devil-may-care adventurer—reminiscent, perhaps, of "Pappy" Boyington and his Black Sheep squadron or the volunteers who flew with the Flying Tigers in China—it nevertheless expresses praise for a brave man from a fellow airman who amply demonstrated his own courage. Indeed, there was a wildness about Diebold. He volunteered to parachute into the jungle within hours of reporting for duty with the 1352nd Search and Rescue Unit in India's Assam Valley. But there is gentleness, too—in the story he tells of nursing a starving native baby—or the sadness of burying a young airman he was too late to save.

Though Diebold died in 1965—his two broken marriages and early death partly the result of his experiences in Burma—he completed the typescript for this book before his life ended. An excerpt had appeared in *Cosmopolitan* magazine shortly after the war and was reprinted in an Army military journal. He wanted to have the account of his rescue operations published as a book, but that never happened. Instead, the typescript languished in the family attic, where for years it was forgotten, gathering dust, until one of his daughters handed it to me.

While not a practiced writer, Diebold does tell a gripping story, all the more immediate because he wrote it shortly after the events he recounts. The book crackles with the language of the time: war slang, wisecracks, and old-fashioned turns of phrase. All work to give it a compelling authenticity. It's also honest. As he might have put it himself, he doesn't pull punches. But it's funny, too, both because he meant it to be and because of occasional tumbles into what he describes as "pure corn."

But more than that, *Hell Is So Green* is an exciting tale. Diebold knew how to tell a story, and that story takes place against a sweeping backdrop of history: the biggest air-supply in history, not surpassed until the Berlin airlift of 1949. In fact, the ATC's supply operation over the Hump made the Berlin airlift possible. It also engaged more than a million Japanese soldiers in China, soldiers who otherwise might have deployed in the Philippines or on Okinawa. His experiences jumping into the jungle also became one of the earliest instances of organized combat search and rescue, a military operation commonplace today.

For some, the CBI theater was a sideshow of the war, a distant third to Europe and the Pacific. But for those who flew the Hump, for those who kept the Dougs flying—Douglas C-46s and C-47s—and for the pilots and crew who had to bail out over terrain as inhospitable as anywhere on the planet, service in the CBI was the greatest challenge of their lives. As it was for Diebold. The heroism that emerges from these pages does so quietly. The story is modestly and self-deprecatingly told. It is only as you read of the heat and stink of the jungle, of the vermin, lice, and leeches, of the towering mountains and roaring rivers, that you begin to realize just what kind of story this is.

Diebold's typescript required some editing, and in the process I found myself expanding his story in minor ways. He was often vague about dates and places; from time to time, he was imprecise or unclear about details or names. Occasionally I had to guess about something he treated unclearly or left unsaid, and I clarified where I could. Such occasions in the book are few and always supported by his family or by documents relating to his war experiences.

Fortunately, Diebold left behind some vivid impressions; several people wrote about him—both during and after the war—and often corroborated or enlarged upon one or another of the stories he tells. I was able to track down details of the air crash that took Diebold out of the war and which brings his tale of jungle rescues to an end. That story, told by an Army reporter writing for the *Hump Express* in May 1945, appears here in the afterword, both to satisfy the curious and to bring Diebold's story to a close.

What follows is almost entirely Diebold's. In the few cases where the manuscript was adjusted, it was to sharpen a point, expand a fact, or to explain a confusing episode. Little has been added because little else was needed, and almost nothing has been removed.

And so, here, out of the shadows and dust of the attic, comes a story of courage in the wild written nearly sixty years ago, but as full of life and high adventure as it was when Diebold first put words to paper.

—Richard Matthews

1

A group of excited young pilots crowded around the desk. I tapped one on the arm and asked what all the fuss was about.

"Here!" he said and handed me a sheet of worn, dirty paper. Laboriously written in a scrawling, unsteady hand were words beginning "Somewhere in Hell . . ."

With difficulty I read the remainder of the note: "I am the pilot who crashed. I need a pair of G.I. shoes, quinine, socks, sulfa for boils and infections rotting my limbs off. I would like to borrow a blanket if you could spare one. Cold. Cigarettes would be nice. I'm ashamed for asking for so much. Thanks for whatever you can do."

The note was signed "Lt. G. M. Collins."

I could see why everyone was so excited; the note packed more wallop than anything I'd ever seen. "That was brought into an airstrip in Burma two days ago by a native," a lieutenant explained. "The native said the pilot is in the Naga Hills, in a village we think is called Geda Ga."

It was the mission, I knew vaguely, of the 1352nd Search and Rescue Squadron to which I'd been temporarily assigned to find downed airmen along the Hump route and rescue them. That's all I did know, though, for I was just this morning reporting for duty. Having arrived the night before at this jumping-off place for China supplies, I was supposed to report immediately to the commanding officer, but given the lateness a sergeant at the airfield had directed me to a hut he called a *basha* and quartered me with fifty other men.

A basha is an American hay mound with doors. The army had gone native: straw roof over a bamboo frame with woven bamboo sides and windows with nothing in them. No glass, no frame, no nothing. They could better be called square holes for ventilation. The one modern touch, cement floors, added little to their attraction. Following a long flight across half of India, I slept well enough that night, though, if I'd known what was in the books for me this morning, there'd have been little sleep.

The inevitable began to kick in when I reported to Major Roland Hedrick, in civilian life a Salt Lake City lawyer.

The major was surrounded by pilots, all talking at once. He was the boss and brains of the outfit, and the pilots were discussing with him—"arguing about" would be more accurate—the note I'd just read. To say I received little attention when I walked into this melee of men puts it mildly; penetrating that circle of gesticulating arms would have been worth a black eye at least.

A pilot near the major made a mountain with one hand, while with the other he imitated an airplane in flight. He was trying to explain how difficult it was to fly around that mountain with the objective of coming low over a native village situated on the mountain's side, near the top. He'd had to come in low over the village, I gathered, to attract the attention of any airman that might be in it. Was the writer of the note in that particular village? Nobody seemed sure.

The major listened patiently enough, but eventually he started chasing off the crowd of officers, moving them gradually toward the door and out into the growing light. One by one they left, each being assured something would be done and that he'd let them know as soon as he knew himself. Figuring he was pretty busy, I turned to leave with them, but, catching my eye, the major indicated I should stay.

"You're Diebold, right?" He stuck out his hand. "Welcome to chaos," he said. "It's not always like this, but we've got a bit of a problem."

Perhaps being a lawyer made the major patient. I don't know what gave him that trait, but now when I think back to that first day I'm happy he had it. I had arrived in India just a few days ago, I didn't know a soul, and frankly I was curious to know what was going on.

We talked about my arrival, I handed him my papers, and he asked me if I'd been able to find a place to sleep. But it was clear I was occupying just a small piece of his mind because he soon drifted into thought, almost as if I wasn't there. Still, he hadn't asked me to leave so I waited. And maybe it was because he needed someone to explain it to one more time that he began telling me what all the pilots had been discussing.

He was confronted with a tough one, he said, a problem that might mean life or death to a pilot. The problem demanded action, but no one seemed to agree what that action should be. I began to realize that his shaking my hand instead of cutting it off showed more patience than I probably deserved.

"Lieutenant, our maps of this wild area show the Naga village of Geda Ga to be here." He pointed to a spot in the mountains of northern Burma. "The boys flew over that village yesterday with two doctors aboard who were ready to parachute out. They weren't able to get down close to the village until late in the afternoon due to the weather. There was a cloud sitting smack on top of that mountain almost all day, and when the cloud finally did move away the boys found two peaks where there should be only one, and damned if there wasn't a village on both peaks."

The major sat back, relit the stub of his old cigar, and pondered for a minute, puffing out evil-smelling smoke which later became, to me, as much a part of him and the outfit as the smell of cooking bacon was part of home.

"The search plane buzzed both spots, dropping notes requesting some kind of signal if the pilot was in that village. Neither village did a thing. Now, we aren't sure which village he's in or even if he's in either. There's a lot of country out there, and we could be mistaken, but I don't think so. I believe the kid, Lieutenant Collins, is too damn sick to get out of the hut and make the signal himself, and he can't make the natives understand what he wants them to do. We've checked on Collins and his P-51 went down more than a month ago. If he's out there, he's probably in a bad way."

The major and I sat in silence, thinking. I had heard a little of the major's reputation before I arrived, and it was all good. A military intelligence officer, he'd been at this sort of work for a long while, and, if he thought the pilot was there, I was inclined to agree with him—but what help could I be?

My eyes drifted to the huge wall map covering one entire side of the room. Different-colored flags were stuck into it, each flag symbolizing a plane on the ground, a crashed plane . . . and there were lots of flags. Later, when the different charts and maps were explained to me, their use became a part of my life, but at that moment they seemed little more than a confusing collection of colors.

"Major," I said, "why couldn't you parachute a man into the village you think most likely to be the right one? If the flyer isn't there, he's bound to be in the other. A process of elimination, as it were."

The major looked at me as if he were seeing me for the first time. "Diebold, that village is hundreds of miles from any semblance of civilization in the toughest kind of jungle. A lot of it's trackless. Hell, a white man goes in there once in twenty years. How would the parachutist get out?"

That stopped me until I happened to think: The downed flyer, a fighter pilot apparently, would have to be brought out and, prior to my question, the major said he'd planned to send in two doctors. He must have had a plan to bring them out.

I said that to him, and we talked about it for a while. He asked me, for instance, what I thought someone jumping into the village might need, whether I thought a person could do it alone, and a few other questions. As he talked, he glanced through my papers. Finally, as if he'd just reached a decision, he agreed what I'd said had merit.

"Except," said the major, "if we're going to give that plan a try, we need someone who will volunteer to jump. And right now we're pretty short-handed."

To this day I'm not entirely sure what Major Hedrick was doing. Mainly he seemed to be trying to convince me how difficult and dangerous such a jump was. But I think he was also sizing me up, trying to get a sense of who I was and what I was willing to do. If that's the case, he was playing it smarter than I was. I was rambling on about parachute jumping and re-supply like I had some idea what I was talking about, but when he said he needed a volunteer to jump I heard my voice say, "Hell, Major, I'll jump."

The statement certainly surprised me and seemed to surprise him as well. For a moment we just looked at each other, and I almost turned around in my chair to see who had just said he'd jump. The silence became uncomfortable as the skipper eyed me long and hard, trying to see, I guess, if I meant what I'd just said.

"Diebold," he said, "you're on temporary duty here, is that right?" I nodded. "You don't come under higher headquarters where I'd normally have to get the O.K. to let you do this, do you?"

"No, sir," I answered. He looked at me again for a minute and then asked, "Would you like to change your mind?"

Everything inside me urged, *Yes, for God's sake, yes*, but I answered, "No."

"All right, boy, go get dressed for a parachute jump and a long trek in the jungle. Be back here in an hour, and I'll get you some gear and fill you in with what you need to know." He paused. "And by the way, welcome to your new home."

I rose from the chair, knees weak, and weaved out of the room I'd so casually walked into less than an hour before and headed for my basha. As I slouched through the mud, my mind was a whirl. The conversation came back to me, like an old jukebox tune I couldn't stop repeating.

What did you wear on a parachute jump, I wondered, or in the jungles and mountains of Burma for that matter? That boy out there needed help from someone, there was no denying that. But why did *I* volunteer?

Well, it might as well be me as anyone else that helps him. And after all, I'm not the first person to try a parachute jump.

But I got little comfort from that. Every third step I kicked myself for being such a fool, even if it might be a lot of fun. *What in the hell made me say it?* I kept thinking. I took a quick look at my life to see if anything there might answer my question.

Four years at Valley Forge Military Academy in Pennsylvania had given me a reserve commission in the cavalry. After that came a series of jobs before I found the right one, and a series of girls before I found a bride. Both the job and the girl I married in Pittsburgh settled the score for me: From there on I was a solid American citizen with a settled future—and a father with a new baby girl. That is, until February 1942, when a letter I received from Uncle Samuel made me a soldier. After that came tours of duty at Fort Riley, Kansas, and other cavalry posts until some general decided we needed gliders to drop soldiers on top of the Germans. Because I'd learned to fly small planes in 1937, I found myself assigned to training that would make me a glider pilot.

Lt. Gene Patterson of Chattanooga, Tennessee, once remarked about that course, and I think he summed it up well: "At night, when you're sitting in that glider at five thousand feet with light rain and winds, and you know in a couple of minutes you're going to reach up and pull the lever that releases your tow line, which leaves nothing between you and that dimly lit field except a pair of wings, good judgment, and a lot of luck—well, a guy must either be crazy or love this goddamn country of ours a hell of a lot to do it."

After glider training, I found myself in the Army Air Corps School of Intelligence. From there, I was stationed in Washington. It was a good tour of duty, and it took me almost a year to catch up on the sleep I lost in that town. What a place!

Then, with typical army logic, after preparing me to drop a plywood glider into Europe, they sent me to jungle school in Panama—rather quick and rudimentary it seemed to me now—and then to the Air Transport Command in India.

Now, in September 1944, at age 27, I was part of the China-Burma-India theater (the CBI in army lingo) and a member of an outfit whose job it was to rescue pilots who had to abandon their ships while flying supplies into China over some of the highest mountains in the world.

No matter how I looked at it as I walked back to my basha, I couldn't find a thing to make me believe I was a young Tarzan. As a matter of fact, I felt like the undertaker could count on me for some quick business—especially in the next few days.

2

My first night in the basha I'd had no opportunity to meet the fellows who lived there, so after my talk with Major Hedrick, I met, for the first time, one of the men.

He slept in the bed next to me, if you want to call them beds. They're what the Indians like, I guess, and have used for centuries. They consist of eight boards, four uprights, and a square. Woven bamboo covers the place that ordinarily would be covered by springs. Sleeping on a washboard would be akin to sleeping on an Indian bed, and the corrugations would be a hell of a lot less numerous. I thought perhaps I might eventually become accustomed to sleeping on them, and it was only the newcomers who felt stiff in the morning. That notion was dissipated now, though, when I watched my next-door bedmate get up. He creaked!

Calisthenics aren't something most of the Army does in their spare time, but with those beds calisthenics are a necessity. That's what my next-door neighbor began doing when I came in; he had to in order to be able to walk. As he unbent from trying to get his muscles back in place, he opened a weary eye and said, "Who the hell are you?"

At the moment I wasn't in the mood for the niceties of social life either, but I stuck out my hand anyway. *Fine reception from the guy you're going to live with*, I thought and said, "My name's Diebold. And who the hell are you?"

He was Lt. Charles King from Scarsdale, New York. Charlie had been flying the Hump most of the night and looked it. With one hand on his hip, as if to keep that bone attached to the rest of his body, he used the other to point in the direction of a bamboo table and two chairs. "Would you care to invest in some furniture?" he asked. "Half of it belonged to the guy who had your bed. I bought it off him when he left."

"O.K., neighbor," I said. "I'll invest when I come back from this trip, if I come back."

"Where are you bound?"

"Well, I'm going to try a parachute jump . . . into Burma."

"Oh," he said, started to tie a shoelace, stopped, looked up, and raised a quizzical eyebrow. "I must be getting old. I thought I heard you say you were going to jump into *Burma*."

"It looks like that's it."

"That's what I thought I heard. And why are you doing that?"

Explaining my meeting with the major, I told him about the downed pilot and confessed that I'd actually volunteered to jump. Charlie sat there for a moment, looking at me, his elbows on his knees, and said, "Christ, whatta way to make a living."

We didn't say much more to each other as I filled my musette bag with things I figured I'd need. I was grateful he didn't bother me with introductions to the rest of the men who lived in the basha as they passed back and forth down the long aisle separating the two rows of beds. Just before I left, though, he gripped my hand hard and said a simple, "Good luck, champ." That felt good. If there ever entered my mind the thought of backing out at the last minute, that thought disappeared then and there.

I spent the next hour with Major Hedrick getting a quick briefing on where I was going and what I needed to know. We looked at the wall map—still largely a puzzle to me—and talked about what supplies I'd need and the support I could expect from the squadron. I was especially glad when he told me that a plane would return to the site after I got on the ground and I could communicate with the crew by radio. I hadn't thought of that, so it came as good news.

Finally he sent me down to squadron operations where a business-like supply sergeant took me under his wing and got me some infantry combat boots to replace the dress shoes I'd arrived in . . . my God, was it just the night before? The boots were more than ankle high and offered support to that most vulnerable part of the body in a jump. He also walked me through the supply depot and helped me select some of the things I'd jump with, explaining that the pilot of the rescue ship would drop more supplies to me as soon as my feet touched the ground. The supply people also gave me a .45 pistol and some silver rupees to pay for anything I might want from the natives—and we were off.

We flew in a Douglas C-47, a version of the DC-3, the same ship used as a passenger liner in the States, only this one had the rear door off and was loaded with para-packs containing food, clothing, and medical supplies. One of the packs, I'd been told, contained a small radio. As the ship took off, I sat on the floor by the open door and watched the ground pull steeply away. The thought struck me that the next time I'd see the ground this close again I would either hit it "splash" or harder than I wanted to hit it. Either way left me little room for comforting thoughts.

We flew for a few hours, and I had a chance to see the country. I wish they had blindfolded me; I would have been happier.

The mountains, of which there were very many, seemed to go straight up and down; if these were the Naga "Hills" they sure had a funny notion of hills in this part of the world. The country was also incredibly green. It wasn't often I could see the ground; the foliage was too thick for that. A solid canopy of jungle stretched in every direction. In my mind's eye I could almost see the snakes sticking their heads out of trees, licking their chops, smacking their lips, if snakes have such things. What did they have in the jungle here? Cobras? I could also hear the tigers telling their cubs to be quiet, that the Army Air Corps was providing them with their supper that night. I was not in a happy frame of mind.

Eventually the pilot called me forward. "Diebold, you've used a parachute before, haven't you?"

What a laugh! The only thing I'd ever used a parachute for was a cushion to sit on in a glider. But I answered, "Not this paratrooper chute you've rigged up for me." Which was true, in a sense.

"Well," he said, "glad to know you. My name's Anderson, Andy to you. From Texas."

"Pleasure," I murmured, not meaning it in the least.

"I've never used one of those either," he said, "but one thing I do know is that you'd better be sure your static line is attached to that cable running along the top of the fuselage back there. I saw a newsreel once of some paratroopers jumping, and that's the way they did it."

Simple, I thought, *now I just have to find out what a static line is*. And as for the pilot's experience in pushing people out of airplanes, the fact that all he knew about it was from watching the movies didn't exactly fill me with confidence.

Eventually we came to the section of the country where our downed pilot was supposed to be. What a country! If a glacier made these mountains it must have been mad as hell at something. They were the biggest, highest hunks of earth I have ever seen piled in one place. When I thought of climbing around in them, they grew even larger and more formidable.

Anderson found the villages, then flew me from them to the Ledo Road, showing me the way out. It looked simple. There couldn't be more than two mountain ranges towering some two miles up apiece, or more than a hundred miles of solid jungle. Nothing to it! We buzzed the villages a couple of times, and it was some of the best flying I've ever seen done, thank God! First we dived down the side of one mountain, gaining excess air speed, and then shot up the side of an adjacent mountain. It would have been lots of fun if I didn't have to jump out of the ship on one of those shoots up the mountainside.

When I'd talked with the major, he said he hoped this second fly-over would give us an idea of which village the pilot was in, but no matter how close we came to the roofs of the houses—and the pilot came damned close—the only thing we saw were wildly waving natives. No parachute, no panel, no signal of any sort. I began to doubt if our pilot was in either of them, but the only way to find out was still the same as it was before: jump in and look.

Finally, as I knew it must, the time came to go. Pretty much at random we picked one of the villages, and Anderson described how the jump would work. He told me to stand at the rear door, and when the bell rang that was my signal to jump. The walk from the pilot's compartment to the rear of that ship was the longest I've ever made.

Sgt. Stanley Bloom from Boston, Massachusetts, helped me into my chute, showed me how to hook up to my static line, and I took my stand at the door. I could feel my heart thudding against my chest as I looked out. It was so far down to the rushing ground, and it was thick and rough. The village sat in a small clearing—very small from the airplane—but all around it was jungle. I could picture my chute being collapsed by one of the top branches of a tall tree, letting me freefall a hundred feet or so.

It seemed I stood there forever, scared to death! I was afraid even to think about it. I did think of my civilian insurance company and its directors, though. Wouldn't they be the happy lot if they could see me now? Once, back when I was a happy civilian, they insisted I stop flying because it was too great a risk for my insurance. Good God, how would they feel about this? Then the bell rang!

I had been waiting unconsciously for that sound, so it took no planned action on my part to get me out that door. I'd conquered my mind when I stepped up to it, and from then on leaping out was reaction to a sound. I'm sure of this, for I can't remember jumping. The bell rang, and the next thing I knew was the roaring of the slip-stream in my ears, the tumbling of the horizon, the tail of the ship passing overhead . . . and then the almighty jerk.

I'd learned to jump the hard way. Body position in the air was an unknown to me, so mine almost certainly was wrong. Also, my chute harness had been cinched too loose, so I got a terrific jerk. I blacked out for an instant, I guess, for the next thing I knew I was alone in the air, all was quiet and serene, and the airplane was gone.

The feeling of elation and exhilaration that came over me when I looked up and saw that big white canopy is indescribable. The chute had opened. Oh, happy day! I kicked my legs, waved my arms, and wiggled my body to make sure nothing had been broken. Nothing had.

I was uncomfortable, though. I'd been jerked down in the too-loose harness, and my entire weight was being carried in the crotch of my legs. It was then, for the first time, that I thought of the ground. Good lord, how it seemed to be rushing up at me. Around the village the natives had cleared the trees from a spot of ground that looked to be about the size of a quarter from the air. It looked larger now, and I could see the clearing was covered with jagged-edged stumps. I wanted to slow my rate of fall but was helpless; all I could do was sit in the harness and wait. I wondered what it felt like to hit the ground as hard as I was obviously going to hit it. A broken leg out here would really be something to worry about. Also, what good would I be able to do anybody if I couldn't walk?

I didn't have to worry long at the rate the ground was coming up to meet me, for that's exactly the way it looks. You have no sensation of falling; it just seems like the ground is being jacked up to your height by some gigantic force that is doing it all too swiftly.

Anderson had done a swell job. As he had planned it, I was going to land in the clearing; the least I could do was miss the stumps. I pulled a handful of shroud lines on my right to see which way it made me go, but it didn't seem to change a thing except to make the ground come up even faster. That was all the argument I needed. Let fate take its course, I wasn't fooling around with those lines any more.

Fate took its course, and I landed bang on top of a stump. It was lucky I did, though, because my knees collapsed, and I bounced, fairly gently, to the ground. The stump broke my fall, and I was relaxed when I hit the earth. Since trees surrounded the clearing, there was no wind, and the chute collapsed without dragging me.

And I was down! For a moment I just sat there saying over and over, aloud, "Goddamn it, I made it." Then I started to laugh at myself, a giddy laugh of relief. I laughed till the tears rolled down my face, I was just too damn happy to be alive.

Then Andy woke me up. (I was willing to think of him as Andy now that I was safe on the ground. In the airplane he'd been a guy named Anderson who wanted to shove me out the door; now he was my link with civilization.) He brought that ship right down in the clearing with me, rolling it over on its side so he could see me. I managed a pretty feeble wave of the arm, and he must have seen it since he went back upstairs and circled, waiting for me to get oriented.

I got up, climbed out of the harness, reached in my pocket, and got a cigarette. My hands were shaking as I lit it. No cigarette ever tasted better.

I was gathering up my chute when I heard them. I couldn't see them, but I could hear them. They were shouting "O.K.—O.K." I stopped, turned in wonderment. "Well I'll be damned," I said aloud, "These people speak English."

Out of the brush they came, three natives. To me they looked pretty fierce; to them I must have looked about the same, for they stopped dead. With one hand on my .45 just for the comfort it brought me (not that I could hit anything with it) I looked them over, two men and a boy. Dressed in loincloths with long knives in their hands, they were brown and small and wiry.

We might have stood there for hours looking one another over, but with that plane overhead I needed to get moving. Looking braver than I felt, I walked over to them.

Since they had said "O.K." coming up the trail, I figured they could speak my language well enough for conversation, so I said, "Well, how the hell are you?"

Their answer was little better than silence: It was "Umm."

I tried again. "Would you like a cigarette?" On that one I did better; they said, "Umm, umm." But when I held out the pack, they took not one cigarette, but the whole damn pack. At least it was action. I tried a little Hindustani I had learned. I put the emphasis on "little," because I knew one word. I asked, "Mullen English?" They said, "O.K."

This could go on all day, I thought. Then I said to them, "Everything's O.K. with me, too."

What I said must have meant something to them (maybe it was the "O.K." part) or else they were tired of our little game. They took my parachute out of my arms and, as if I were a little child, led me by the hand down the trail. The only thing that reassured me they weren't leading me to the slaughter was the big smile I got from the little boy when he lit his cigarette.

Andy had begun buzzing the village when I arrived there. It felt good, actually, to have him overhead, flying around and making noise. It seemed to lend importance to who I was. The village consisted of just two houses, and everybody turned out to see me come in. I took out a white cloth and waved it to the plane to let them know I was in the pink. I guess they misunderstood me, though, because on the next trip around, before I had time to see if the pilot was in either of the houses, they started dropping supplies.

When that outfit drops supplies, they really do it! In less time than it takes to tell, the sky filled with billowing parachutes, and the natives and I ran for cover. Stanley Bloom up in that aircraft was pushing them out three at a time. Each pack weighed about a hundred pounds and wasn't exactly the thing to be hit with, and they were dropping everywhere. When our aerial pounding ended, I wondered what I'd done to make Andy want to kill me. Luckily none of the natives had been hit, or their houses.

On one pack, painted in large letters, was RADIO. I opened it, took out the handie-talkie, and pulled out the aerial. Immediately Andy's voice came over the air in the midst of a conversation that went something like this: "... Diebold will probably be barbecued tonight." It made me feel swell. The story back at the squadron held that these people had been headhunters in the past, but this was now, and things like that don't happen any more (it says here in small print).

"Andy," I said into the mike, "one more crack like that and I will name my next six Naga children after you." All I heard from the other end of my radio was a squawk, then in a clearer voice, "Is he there, Bill?"

"How the hell should I know? I just got here myself. Take it easy, my boy, take it easy, and I'll find out. Old cutthroat here should know."

I turned to the native who was looking at me as if I were crazy, standing there talking into a box. I pointed to myself and said, "American," then pointed to the two houses and asked, "American?" He shook his head in the negative, a surprise since I had expected little from my first try. Then the native babbled excitedly to his kinfolk who by this time were standing around in a close circle, staring. They babbled back at him, and then he turned to me. He pointed to the opposite mountain where the other village sat and said something like, "Amoodicaun," over and over.

"You don't have to hit me with an oak tree; I got it." The fellow I was looking for was in the other village. My luck was as usual! It never fails to happen. If I had bailed out in the other village, I'd bet my bottom dollar they would have moved him to this one the day before.

I got on the air. "Andy."

"Air to gravel-shuffler, go ahead. What gives?"

What a character that guy was, but I gave him the dope. "Right girl, wrong night, my boy. Come back tomorrow, and I'll be next door with the body."

Andy's voice came back: "You're in, sleep tight. See you at the next mountain tomorrow. There's a bottle of medicinal alcohol in one of those packs—I'll be back sometime tomorrow afternoon. If there's nothing else you need, this is Andy saying adieu to you."

And that was it.

3

I watched the big plane disappearing over the far mountain with definite misgivings. It made me lonely just to see it go. There I stood in the middle of a group of staring natives . . . and all I could think to do was stare back at them.

The women wore clothes, damn it. Wrapped around their middles were long pieces of varicolored cloth. Around their breasts they wore a plain piece of dirty white cloth or another piece matching the skirt. They all wore necklaces, made of anything from animal teeth on a string to old coins or pieces of metal. The men, most of them, wore nothing but a loincloth, and others had the same wrapping the women wore around their waists.

What surprised me most was their hair. Both men and women alike wore it up, piled on top of their heads. If it weren't for the very definite outline of women's bodies, I would have been bewildered as to which sex was which. As it was, nature provided the curves.

Well, we couldn't stand there staring at one another forever, so I took an important step: I smiled. There was one old geezer the others seemed to treat with respect who I had already guessed was the head man. On top of that, he had some sort of feather in his hair none of the others had. Either the others had lost theirs, or it meant something. I gave him the old try; I smiled directly at him.

He nodded his head a couple of times and gave me what I took to be a tentative smile in return. With that, I felt on more solid ground and decided to try to get things in hand. Scattered all over the clearing were the white para-packs. Some were even in the trees at the edge of the clearing. The kids of the village were beginning to poke experimental noses into their contents, and I could picture the results if they started opening them and spreading their contents all over the area. Best to get them gathered up and at least stacked in a pile where I could keep an eye on them.

I looked at the feather-headed village elder, smiled again, and gave him another cigarette from my last pack—there were more in the dropped supplies, I knew, which was another reason to get them secured. I pointed to the various para-packs and then to one of their houses. He must have understood what I meant because he barked out some orders, and in a flash the packs were being gathered up by the natives. The chief, if that's what he was, led me to one of the houses while this was going on.

What a place those houses were. Built on stilts about ten feet off the ground, they were long, bamboo-woven things with grass roofs. In front, they actually had a porch.

Very civilized, I thought, but later I learned the hard way about the porches' uses.

The chief and I wallowed through the mud to his house. I called it mud, with a mental frown, for surrounding the house were two or three water buffalo and a dozen or so animals that slightly resembled pigs. *Ah, the beautiful odors of a Naga village* I thought as I followed the chief along. We entered his house via a fancy stairway made from a log with notches cut into it for steps. I wondered how my old Naga friend made it up that log on his night out; that is, if his wife gave him a night out.

The inside of the hut resembled a large communal basha, not unlike the one back at the base, though more worn with use. Several rooms ran to the rear of the shack, all connected to each other so that to go to the rearmost room, one had to walk through the sleeping quarters of everyone in the house. The front room looked like the natives' version of a living room or parlor. In the rear of the room a small fire flickered in the center of the floor on sand or something. But what stopped me cold were the decorations on the walls. On every wall hung a heterogeneous collection of dried heads. On some the skin had turned to a brown parchment-like covering. Others were nothing but the grinning, white skull. Though they were almost certainly animal skulls, one look at those and I wanted to move out of there in high gear.

Every kind of head imaginable hung in the shadows. The heads that were simply skulls really frightened me. The open holes that were once eyes, combined with the absence of any lower jaw, gave them a lurid expression.

They looked as if they were smiling to me in an open invitation to join them in their vigil.

On one wall were the skulls of huge water buffalo, horns still intact. On another were the skulls of large birds, probably vultures. The long beaks protruded from the skull, and here and there I could see tufts of hairy fuzz.

What really made me gulp and thank Mr. Colt for inventing our .45 automatic were the monkey heads. I've been told since then, by men who should know, that they were monkey heads and not human. But from where I was standing they looked like the largest monkey heads I'd ever seen. They came awfully close to looking like what I thought mine probably looked like under the skin. I began to pick the spot where they'd probably put mine. At least I wanted a good spot, overlooking the porch.

The chief beckoned me over to the fire. I wasn't cold but I thought it a good idea, in view of the heads, to play ball with him. After all, I kept telling myself, I was his guest; morale and good relations, you know, are a lot of little things.

The chief sat cross-legged on the floor and motioned me to join him. He then pulled out a two-foot-long, two-inch-diameter pole made of bamboo, filled it with water, dropped in some brown stuff, put one end in the fire, and propped the other end against a forked stick. We were going to have tea, cooked in bamboo. It was almost too much. *The prisoner ate a hearty meal before . . .*

Our fire was very smoky, and there was no chimney. I watched the smoke curl up as the chief blew on the fire to make it hot. First the smoke filtered through a series of bamboo layers hanging from vines from the thatched roof. On some layers of bamboo lay meat; on others, nothing. The ones with nothing on them, I later learned, were drying and would be burned in the fire. On the others, the meat looked delicious.

I learned later that when bamboo was used in the fire, the meat was moved out of the smoke. My first lesson in jungle lore: There must be undesirable gases in bamboo smoke. After passing over the meat and helping dry extra bamboo for the fire, the smoke curled on up to the peak of the roof, followed the peak to the end of the house, and there dissipated into the outside air. As the smoke ran along the roof it blackened the straw, or whatever it was that covered the house. Every so often a big hunk of this soot would fall down on my head and the heads of the natives, which they casually brushed off.

The chief had poured water for the tea from fat bamboo logs racked in a row behind him. These were kept constantly full by the women. The nearest water being at the foot of the mountain, they had to make that hike a couple of times a day. Coming up with their backs loaded down with water-filled bamboo gave them a beautiful carriage, and strong legs—and, as I was to learn tomorrow, made them a lot tougher than they looked.

We had our tea from bamboo cups. That tea was so strong it snarled at me as I tried to swallow it. These natives, I decided, had galvanized stomachs. The stuff tasted like boiled tobacco. Nevertheless, I nodded, smiled, and smacked my lips in evident enjoyment. This pleased the chief, I was happy to see, and he, too, smiled, smacked his lips, and said something like "Kajaiee." I treasured the word as my first. It must mean good, although at the taste of the tea, I could hardly believe it.

By this time, the natives outside had piled up all the para-packs. I stood on the porch with the chief and looked at them in dismay. There were so many and all in the wrong village, and I wished Andy hadn't been so hasty in dumping them out of the plane. How I was ever going to get them from where they were over to the far mountain where they should be was beyond me.

It was now late afternoon and too late to try and make the trek to the other village. The jungle looked tough enough in the daytime, and it didn't take a lot of imagination to guess it could be deadly at night. I went down in the mud and lifted all the packs up on the porch. I was amazed to find that one of these native boys could carry one of those packs on his back, as they had done to get them in the pile, but it took three of them to lift one up. My hoisting them onto the porch caused no end of consternation among them. It gave them a mistaken estimate of my strength, which I was to become all too unhappy about the next day on the trail. Up on the porch again, I opened one of the packs and found a couple of cartons of cigarettes. I passed a few cigarettes around to the boys who had brought in the packs. They seemed tickled as hell. It made me think of the number of servants a man could have in that country for a buck a month.

My problem was to get as much of this stuff over to the next mountain as possible. I looked at the chief, pointed to one of the packs, then to the other mountain, and made a couple of motions as if I were carrying one of the packs and walking. Then I pointed to the handful of men below us. It seemed an impossible job. Those few men could never, even if they wanted, carry all this equipment.

Evidently the chief got the idea for he smiled, nodded, said, "Kajaiee," and called one of the older boys up on the porch. They held a lengthy conversation while I stood looking, wondering what the hell was going on. At the end of the conversation, the boy crawled off the porch and, with another companion, started down the trail. Was he being sent for more help? All I could do was to hope for the best.

We went back inside, for more tea I presumed, and sat down by the fire. They did pour more tea and then sat back contentedly smoking their cigarettes. I decided there would just have to be a stop to this tea drinking; I couldn't stand the gaff. Then I remembered what Andy had said about the bottle of medicinal liquor. After what I had been through that day I felt I wouldn't be cheating Uncle Sugar too much if I had a drink or two before dinner, so I found the bottle and did. It was damn good bourbon and was easier to swallow than the native's tea had been, but it also made me realize I was hungry.

I found some rations and started to cook a little dinner over the native's fire. I say dinner, but it consisted mostly of cereal because the rations consisted mostly of cereal. It wasn't what I would usually order for dinner, but, compared to what the Naga chief offered, the cereal looked delicious. His menu, deluxe style, consisted of monkey meat, which was cooked before my eyes. They tossed a dead monkey, whole and entire, into the fire.

The chief, after he had eaten, took out a long bamboo pipe. About a third of the way up the pipe from the bottom, an inch-thick piece of hard vine stuck out. He poured water into the mouth of the pipe, held it upright, and then lay down on the floor. In one hand he had a copper dish with a long handle. In this he put a brown pasty substance. He held this over the fire until the brown stuff came to a sizzle. At the same time he had shredded a green, folded leaf with his knife. He browned the shreds in front of the fire. When they were good and brown, he mixed the sizzling stuff into it. All these elaborate troubles were for what? Was he going to smoke the stuff or eat it?

When the mixture was cooked to his satisfaction, he put it in the vine sticking out of the bamboo. Now I was really puzzled! I've watched a lot of people smoke pipes, but this was the damnedest conglomeration of tobacco or anything else I'd ever seen. I didn't really know that he was smoking opium, but I soon guessed when I saw the beatific look on his face, the utter relaxation of his body, and the "out of this world" look in his eyes. I was surprised, but I wasn't shocked, not after these many years in the Army. Everyone had their own way of getting tight—even if this one was a bit unusual. It certainly seemed to agree with him; he looked so happy, so self-satisfied that I almost envied him. And he wasn't alone, for on all sides of me, the boys were reaching with bamboo tongs for embers out of the fire to light their own pipes. This was going to be quite a party.

I had my choice: either go to bed or have a couple more drinks of medicinal liquor. (The chief had his vice; I had mine.) This opium den held quite a bit of interest, though, so I decided I'd stay up and see how it ended. Anyway, it was darn good liquor. After a few more, the party seemed to be getting dull. Then a song, for no reason I could think of, came out of nowhere into my head, "Old McDonald Had a Farm." It seemed lively enough for the occasion, anyway, so I sang a couple of verses, and it wasn't long until a few natives began chiming in "E-I-E-I-O." Soon they were all doing it, with real gusto, and we had ourselves a chorus.

But after a couple thousand "Old McDonald"s I figured we'd disturbed the jungle enough, and I decided to go to bed. The bourbon had been so good I'd completely forgotten it was at all unusual to be singing in a shack on a mountain in the middle of the Burmese jungle with a bunch of opium-drunk natives. But at the time it all seemed rather natural.

I walked out to the porch and to the para-packs. One of those fool bags had my bed in it, but which one? I tried the one on top, and my luck was good. In it was a jungle hammock, which I'd never used, but it came with directions. The directions went something like this: "Find two trees, ten to fifteen feet apart . . ." etc. In the dark I had little desire to go wandering in the jungle looking for two trees ten to fifteen feet apart, but in the hut there was nothing even remotely resembling two trees. Then I remembered the uprights supporting the porch. *Just the spot*, I thought. As I fell down the niched log stairway and picked myself out of the mud, I decided Charlie King had been right, there had to be a better way to make a living.

With a flashlight in one hand, directions in the other, and the hammock between my legs, I tried to figure out how it should be put up. Two of these poles under the porch should do it.

The two end ropes I tied to the poles. Then there was the little matter of the mosquito netting that surrounded the hammock and attached to it. At each of the four corners the manufacturers had put a small cord. I tied these to the lattice-work the natives had covering their porch. The whole thing, as I stood back and surveyed my work, made quite a nest.

But when I tried to get into it, it wouldn't stop swinging. A zipper ran the entire height of the mosquito netting with another joining it that ran half the length of the hammock. I tried to crawl through the hole made by the two zippers and somehow made it, but when I was in, I found I'd forgotten to remove my boots. With the type of mud surrounding that hut, removing them was a necessity. I slowly reached down to get them off—a move I shouldn't have tried because I became tangled in the blankets. I guess I was twisting and turning more than the manufacturers of the hammock had foreseen, and I capsized, ending up lying on the part that should have been over my head.

It looked to me like the best thing I could do was get out and start all over, but how? The hammock was swinging furiously back and forth, tossing me around inside like a squirrel in a bag. I'll never know how I got my body out of the torture chamber, but eventually I stood in the mud and looked at the twisted, impossible mess that was supposed to be my bed.

So I started again. I had to sleep somewhere. But how was I to get my boots off and get through the hole without putting my stocking feet in the mud? I tried sitting on the edge and removing them, but it was like sitting on a swing and trying to remove one's shoes. Naturally I ended up standing in the mud in my stocking feet. By this time I was so angry I didn't care how I got into it or where I slept, on the sides, bottom, or top of the hammock. I was sweating, breathing hard, and covered with mud.

The solution turned out to be simple: I dived at the hammock's opening and made it, though it took a second to stop revolving, but eventually the hammock and I ended our struggle right side up. Even so, the blankets were wound around my body so tightly I could hardly move, the mosquito netting was in my mouth, and my feet were wet and muddy. I had also forgotten to take off my web belt so my canteen was jabbing me in the back and my .45 was making a poor impression on my ribs. To top it off, I wanted a cigarette.

Slowly, so as not to upset my precarious equilibrium, I stalked the cigarette pocket with one hand, clutching the side of the hammock with the other. Somehow I got the pack out of my pocket without upsetting the whole works, got the cigarette lit without setting fire to the hammock, and settled back, exhaling a cloud of smoke and listening to the jabbering of the natives in front of their fire. It occurred to me that the bourbon (together with some of the wayward opium smoke) might possibly have contributed to my struggles with the bedding, but I dismissed the idea as unlikely.

It seemed a beautiful night now that I had stability. Surrounding our mountain were other giants of this country, each outlined in cloaks of mist and moonlight. It would have been eerie had it not been for the billion stars surrounding a huge yellow moon. It was so peaceful I almost forgave the man who had invented the jungle hammock.

On a far mountainside, a jackal raised its voice; a nearer one answered. The sound drifted to my ears out of the mist. With the flicker of the fire inside the hut and the voices of the natives, the jackal didn't scare me much. When I became convinced the animal wasn't under my bed, I relaxed again. It was still a beautiful night.

The natives continued to talk, and it wasn't long until I could recognize the different voices. The words were impossible to understand except for one which sounded like they might be trying to say, "American." I didn't care much for that; it seemed to me little good could come out of their becoming too curious about me. One voice rose above the others, and every third word seemed to be "American," and I worried a little more. The less I entered into their conversation, the better I liked it, since I could still close my eyes and picture those heads on their wall. The hair on the back of my neck crawled at the thought. I grabbed my .45 and with a trembling hand took a firm grip on it. Of course the natives were never safer than when I had that gun, but I was hoping they wouldn't know that.

As the conversation increased almost to shouting, one of the natives walked out on the porch and looked down at me. With what I hoped was a forceful voice, but was probably little more than a squeak, I asked, "Wonderful night for murder, isn't it?" The character didn't answer. He just stood there in the moonlight looking at me, the fire lighting up one side of his face.

He stared for what seemed like forever; then to my surprise came the sound of running water. I couldn't believe it, but in the moonlight I could see it was true: I was sleeping in the Naga's bathroom and this guy was using it. After the first Naga, came a long procession, all relieving themselves over my bed. I thanked the manufacturer of the jungle hammock for the tarpaulin he had put over the top; otherwise it would have been a very damp night.

4

During the night, dozens of natives entered the village. The two men the chief had sent out earlier evidently had been emissaries to other Naga villages, though God knows where they were in the jungle. The men had done their job well, though. There seemed to be an ample number to carry our equipment the next day.

One thing that interested me no end, and scared me more than a little when I first saw it down the trail, was their version of a flashlight. Having decided I was in no danger from the natives—other than getting peed on—I was lying there relaxed and smoking. As I looked out into the darkness, I saw a small red ball bobbing and weaving in the air. The medicinal liquor had been good, perhaps even better than that, but I hadn't drunk enough to be seeing things that weren't there. But red balls don't appear for no reason. All I could do was sit up in the hammock— as much as I could sit up—and watch them approach. It wasn't really fear that made me shake, I told myself, it was only nervousness. Then, from the faint glow of the balls I glimpsed the human forms behind them. I lay back relieved, for the balls were only the glowing tips on the end of bamboo poles.

Finally I went to sleep. It was a fitful, disturbed sleep filled with little brown men looking down at me through their front porch, peeing into the night, and waving red balls in the air. I seemed to be stuck knee-deep in mud and unable to miss the man-made dew that was falling so heavily. It was not a comfortable night.

If the Naga ever went to bed that night I don't know, but at 4:30 in the morning, while it was still dark, the women were up and pounding something I correctly guessed to be rice. The muffled thud, thud, continuous and without rhythm, would wake a hibernating bear. Shortly thereafter I heard the voices of the men and could see the brightening reflection of their fire. Wearily, I swung my feet out of the hammock, wiggled my mud-caked toes, and eased into my boots.

As I climbed the notched ladder, my eyes met a sight I won't easily forget: The big front room of the chief's house was filled to overflowing with brown-skinned Nagas, all of them staring at me. The fire behind them framed their squatting bodies, their piled up hair, with a flickering, weird background. All I could see was the glint of white teeth and the glitter of eyes. The leering, naked skulls on the wall framed them, and the air was heavy with tobacco smoke, sweaty bodies, and effluvium. Standing at the entrance of that room, I tried to smile and said my one

Naga word, "Kajaiee." It worked. They actually laughed. The tension was broken. The old chief unfolded himself and came forward, took me by the hand, and led me to the fire.

My God, I thought, *not tea, not at this hour!* But tea is what the good and venerable chief had in mind. Holding up both hands to him in a negative gesture, I went to the food sack for some good old American coffee. I didn't know how it would taste cooked in a bamboo tube, but it couldn't be worse than their tea.

Taking a bamboo tube from the rack behind the chief, I poured in some coffee and water, stuck the end of it in the fire, and propped up the other end with a forked stick. At first the chief looked puzzled, then slightly annoyed until I poured him a bamboo cupful and he tasted it. His face lit up in evident enjoyment and he passed the cup around the circle of men. A few were missed, so I put another tube-full on to boil. That was a mistake. In the next half-hour, I did nothing but make coffee for the Nagas. They drank it as fast as I could brew it.

Finally calling a halt to the coffee making, I put water on to boil for cereal. The brightly colored box, proclaiming it the finest cereal in the world, was cause in itself for a murmur of assent from my friends. I cooked more than I could possibly eat since I had a feeling this was going to be a repetition of the coffee incident. It was, but I underestimated the food capacity of a Naga.

Batch after batch of cereal went down those hungry gullets. I wondered what they would have done for food if I hadn't been there to cook breakfast for them. When I finally called a halt to this noise, I sat back and contemplated them with a lifted eyebrow. I looked at my burnt fingers and reflected on the peculiarities of life. *Once was*, I thought, *the wife* . . . but, hell, that was too long ago to remember.

Still, the Naga were very appreciative and smiled their thanks. In a way, I was rather proud of having pleased and filled them, much like the hostess who has spent hours in the kitchen appreciates guests who enjoy the dinner. I leaned against the wall, lit a cigarette, and gazed with warmth upon the recipients of my labors.

But having finished his cereal and understanding I wasn't going to make any more, the chief moved to the fire and began boiling rice—and in huge quantities. It couldn't be! These people were so small and yet had eaten more per capita than is ordinarily consumed by a food-loving American soldier. The shock, so early in the morning, was almost too much. I sat there and watched with awe as those damn natives ate all that rice—and there wasn't a potbelly in the crowd.

By then the dawn was beginning to lighten up the jungle. Red beams poured down the green mountainsides and probed the interior of our hut. In the valleys, a few trees reached through the mist they'd slept under. In the forest, the animals began to stir and yawn. The strange early morning cries of birds mingled with the dog-like bark of deer. *Soon we'll be on our way*, I thought, which proved how little I knew yet about the Nagas.

Fooling around with this and that in preparation for the day's hike, I didn't pay much attention to the chief and his men. I presumed, though, that they, too, were getting ready. But when I finally looked over at them, they were all stretched out around the fire smoking their pipes again. I went over to the chief and made signs like walking and hurry-up and pointed to the mountain he'd indicated yesterday as the one where my flyer was. To my gesticulations the old chief just nodded and smiled in a sapient sort of way . . . and continued smoking his pipe. It was most exasperating. Generations of American habit were ahead of me, which included getting a job done when it needed to be done, but like it or not I would have to wait until they were good and ready to go.

Soon, though, my friends began to stir a little. They'd started opening the para-packs, oohing and aahing at each article they uncovered, from cans of beans to a tube of shaving cream, the latter an item I could have done without. Each of the natives had a little basket which would hold, I imagined, about thirty pounds. The baskets were of a peculiar construction. The top of the baskets had two shoulder straps of woven bamboo, with another strap looping from the top of the basket through a wooden yoke. It looked a little puzzling, until they put them on their backs; then it became a sensible arrangement. They put their arms through the two loops attached to the basket and the yoke fitted on the backs of their necks against their shoulders. The end of the other loop went onto their foreheads. It looked so solid and balanced that they probably could have done somersaults without the baskets falling off.

Gradually their work grew efficient: the men formed a circle, baskets in hand, and the chief loaded them.

Evidently they had union rules, though, for each man was loaded according to his size. The larger a man was, the larger his load. The chief was the big cheese, and there was little or no argument from the men in the circle.

When all of his men had their baskets full, a considerable number of things remained in the packs. The old chief went out and recruited all the youngsters, male and female, plus a number of young ladies. To all of these he gave lighter loads, but it emptied the para-packs completely.

It was a long and colorful line of porters that started down the trail. Interesting, I thought, that a complete stranger could drop out of the sky with enough equipment to fill a large truck and, merely by asking, get so much help and cooperation. So far there had been no question of payment. Either they didn't expect any or I, somehow, was supposed to know what to give them for their work.

Going downhill was fine as far as I was concerned, no effort at all. The jungle was thick, though, with brush close in on all sides and in many places overhead as well. We went through a field of grass that was at least ten feet high. I gawked so much at everything around me that I kept tripping over rocks and roots in the trail. The chief cut me a bamboo stick and, like a blind child, I felt my way along.

But if downhill was O.K., the jungle nearly smothered me, and I could seldom see more than a few feet off the trail. The jungle was a solid mass of vines, trees, and brush all interlaced, forming a solid, almost impenetrable wall.

Then there were the leeches. As I walked down the trail I could see them sitting up, half their bodies waving around in the air, waiting for me to brush them with my foot or leg. When I did, they attached with such tenacity that pulling them off was a terrific job. In the first place, their bodies are covered with slime; to get a grip with my fingernails was next to impossible. Those fool slugs could crawl through the eye of a shoe or between the belt of my trousers and shirt—which some did. When they hit flesh, they sank in their jaws, excreting a fluid that frees blood of its usual ability to coagulate. Then they grew larger and larger as they drank my blood.

If, after they'd sunk their jaws, I tried to pull them off, their jaws remained, poisoning the wound and causing infection. One leech wouldn't have been hard to deal with, but the jungle was full of them, and they attached themselves by the dozens. They hung from trees, they were on the brush that whipped by bare arms on the trail, they lay in wait in the mud. If a man should lie down on the grass for very long without taking precautions, the leeches would certainly have him.

But I only began to be aware of the leeches gradually and especially after I noticed that after about ten minutes of walking the Naga would stop and pick something off their bodies. Though I couldn't feel anything biting me, I began to look myself over. *My God*, I thought as I saw them on my legs. *I'm establishing a leech-head in Burma.* They were all over me. I tried to flick a few of the crowd off, but they'd catch onto my fingers and hang on. It was like trying to throw away chewing gum.

As I struggled, more climbed up my legs from the ground. I was being swamped with leeches. It made me almost panic-stricken; I wanted to run, to do anything to escape these weird, disgusting organisms. They turned what looked like a tropical walk in the woods into a nightmare. From there on, I, too, stopped every few minutes and pulled leeches. The natives in their bare feet and loincloths could see all the leeches that landed on them. Earlier I had thought of the Naga as nearly naked; now I thought of myself as over-clothed. With all my clothing, I was at a disadvantage, and it worried me to think about the ones I couldn't see that were drinking away.

At the foot of the mountain we came to a river, a roaring torrent of water, all the more surprising because the thick growth had muffled its sound until we were almost upon it. The mountainside swept straight down to the stream, and at first it seemed impassable. But the trail had been chosen with care. Behind a huge boulder in the stream was a comparatively quiet pool, and in a second the men had stripped and were in it. The women, too, showed no hesitation as they joined in the swim.

The bath had a two-fold purpose: It was fun, and it washed off the leeches. Slightly abashed, I stripped and joined them. Women or no, the leeches had to go. When I took off my trousers I saw my legs were covered with the fat and blood-swollen creatures. The Nagas stopped their splashing and helped me pick them off my naked body. My crimson face, I guess they thought, must be getting sunburned.

By now the early coolness had passed. The sun was hot, and the cold water tumbling down out of some high place was refreshing. It was fun to stand there and watch these primitive people, unaffected by civilization, relax and enjoy themselves. But it was clear we had to move on. If the poor guy in the village we were making for was in serious shape, minutes might count. This time, though, I took a hint from these "primitives" and started out in nothing more than my shorts and boots. After all, this was their country, and being nearly naked had obvious advantages.

So out of the water and up the mountain we started, and with each step uphill—and each new leech—it became hotter and hotter. The Naga are hill people, and hills are their business, but with me . . . well, hills are wonderful when you're flying over them or walking down them, but the Naga build their trails straight up and down a mountain. The trail went up in front of my face. If I stuck out my tongue, I could have picked up a leech or two on it; and why not? They were everywhere else! I began using both hands and feet to make the grade.

For a while we followed the bed of a small secondary stream tumbling down the hill. The water rushing against my unsteady feet on the slippery rocks made walking not only difficult but hazardous. Where the bank of the stream was steepest was where the Naga, naturally, chose to climb out. We clambered along a slippery mud path for a while, sliding back half a step for every one we moved forward. Then we came to a fallen tree slanted upward across what looked like a shallow depression in the ground. Though the log's surface was covered with slippery moss, the Naga with their bare feet walked along it with ease. Then I tried it. It didn't look too bad: even if I did slide off, the ground below me was covered with foliage, or so I thought. About halfway up the log, my feet started slipping, and off I went, right through the foliage under which I expected to find the ground—but the ground was another ten feet down. The log had covered an over-grown ravine.

I landed stunned and bruised and a little shaken. My friend the chief threw me a vine and hauled me out, a somewhat embarrassed jungle novice. None of the Naga who were watching the performance laughed; I would have felt far better if they had. To the contrary, they seemed upset about the whole thing, which puzzled me. The next log we came to like that one, they all stopped, lay down their packs and built a bamboo railing for me. I felt rather silly but a hell of a lot safer, and I began to realize they were concerned that this big dumb American might hurt himself and ruin the whole trip.

On and on we chugged up the mountain, the hill people keeping up a running conversation as they climbed. I was thankful I was still able to breathe. Every cigarette I ever smoked came back to haunt me. The chief in front of me actually stopped once, lit an old pipe, and continued up the hill. How he did it I'll never know. The odor of that foul tobacco whipping past my nose cut down considerably on my oxygen supply.

It seemed forever, but we finally hit the top. And perched up there was a village, if I may call one house a village. I looked around for the lost pilot, but of course this wasn't the right village; we still had another mountain to climb.

By now it was around noon, and the sun was really pouring it on. The water in my canteen was about to boil—so was my blood, what blood the leeches had left me. All the

Nagas jabbered to each other, and I staggered under the shade of the house. When I finally got the sweat out of my eyes enough to see, I lit a cigarette and looked around.

As soon as I did that, though, I had to pass cigarettes out to all the party. There went another pack. *The money I could make as a cigarette salesman out here after the war*, I thought as I passed them around to eager hands. Everyone quietly sat down for a smoke except one woman who stood in front of me holding a baby in her arms.

The baby was a cute little thing, except where there should have been hair there was nothing but a mass of scabs and running sores. Some of the scabs were dry and puckered and must have hurt the baby like hell. It was almost unimaginable to me, raised in America, that there should be a place where babies were raised without proper medical attention. I felt for the child and, though no doctor, thought there must be something I could do to help.

The mother handed me the baby, and, showing him a small bandage I carried that had a red cross on it, I asked the chief for the medical kit. He got the idea, unpacked a couple of baskets, and found it. First I washed the child's head with warm water and then smoothed the whole thing with boric acid ointment. I remembered that a doc had once used boric acid in my eyes, so I knew it probably wouldn't be too strong for the baby's tender skin. The salve I knew was needed to soften the scabs and relieve the pain, but that's about all I knew. I gave the mother a can of it and, through signs, was able to make her understand to put some on twice a day and to keep the child out of the sun.

All this treatment, though, must have given the Naga the impression I was a medicine man, for they all crowded around, each with a complaint. Here, I guess they thought, was a man who could help them with their aches and pains at last. My presence took on a new meaning for them, and they began clamoring for attention. Being human, I couldn't resist the temptation; also, I figured I could at least help them more than if they had no treatment at all. Naga after Naga came forward, many with the same trouble, infected leech bites. They were rather vicious-looking things in their later stages. Some of the holes looked like volcanoes and bore down to the bone. I opened each one with a sterilized knife, swabbed it clean, applied sulfa powder, and wrapped it with a bandage. I was doubtful about how much good I was doing, but it was at least an effort in the right direction. They all seemed satisfied with my treatment, though, for they went away smiling.

So far, I had been the great white savior, that is until a case appeared that stopped me cold. A woman made her way over to me. She tapped her chest below the breast and grimaced. She was older than some of the girls and rather heavy, and her trouble might have been any number of things. But so as not to lose face with my new crowd of patients, I put on my best professional air: I thumped her chest with one hand tapping the other, put my head down as I had seen doctors do, and listened with an intent expression. Actually I couldn't hear a thing except one hand tapping the other, but I could see the Naga watching in wonderment.

After three or four thumps, I raised my head as if I had found the solution, a smile of assurance playing around my mouth. But the solution I'd found was to my trouble, not hers, for my eye had caught the caption on one of the bottles in the medical kit. It said "bicarbonate of soda, peppermint flavored." I solemnly unscrewed the top, handed her a couple of tablets, and told her to chew them by putting an imaginary pill in my mouth and chewing vigorously. The old gal put the two I'd handed her into her mouth and chewed. The effect was immediate: After rice all her life, the peppermint must have tasted swell. Her face lit up with evident enjoyment. From there on, after she told the rest, I had a dozen cases of chest pains, and my bottle was soon empty.

Other cases came forward as well—various infected cuts, punctures, and sores, and I fixed them all up, one after another. I was making friends by the dozen, and, frankly, I felt sorry for them. And, curiously, I began feeling friendship toward them as well; the fact is, I was learning to like these people. I liked them for their toughness and their willingness to help, for their friendliness and enthusiasm and quickness to smile, and for the way they trusted this oversized American stranger who had entered their lives by dropping out of the sky.

Eventually we started out again. Though I still felt the urgency of getting to the pilot, by now I wasn't in so much of a hurry. My muscles ached, and my head swam. The thought of another grueling climb like that last mountain nauseated me. But off we went.

What goes up must go down, thank the Lord, because for us it was now down, but so steep and muddy that I spent most of my time sliding on what was left of my undershorts. The stones didn't bother my posterior much; it was the sharp roots that did it. Still, we made good time and soon reached another river. This one wasn't as large as the last one, but it was just as welcome. To the natives, who obviously knew this stream was coming, the trip down didn't seem so bad, but to me, who could see another half a day ahead with nothing but leech bites and the sweltering heat, it seemed longer than it was.

We shed our clothing again, and in we went. I took a moment to look at my feet, though, and they seemed like bloody stumps. Blisters everywhere. Then, when I jumped into the pool, damned if I didn't get almost swept downstream with the current. Going under, I grabbed the nearest hand. When I got back onto my feet and blew the water out of my lungs, I was able to mutter a meek "kajaiee." I looked at the person whose hand I had grabbed and who was now holding me up, and my face turned crimson; the big strong hero had been saved by a gal half his size . . . and she wasn't hard on the eyes either. Mumbling at the vagaries of fate, I felt like a country bumpkin, but she smiled at me as if she saved stupid Americans every day. I smiled back . . . and we began to pick leeches off each other. It was fascinating, too, to see where a quick-eyed girl with nimble fingers could think of to look for leeches. I was becoming accustomed to this primitive way of life and began to think it an inviting way to live.

The stream, of course, was at the bottom of the mountain we'd just descended, but to me it had been the top of the day. But from here on it was up, up, forever up. I was so slow that even the women, burdened as they were with packs, pulled away from me. I just couldn't keep up. No longer was I walking: Stumbling and struggling were more the words for it. Climb a hill for an hour, most of us can do, but when it comes to climbing them all day—give me a streetcar. Two hours after we left that stream, I was about finished. I kept thinking of Rudyard Kipling's poem "If." The line kept running through my head—"And so hold on when there is nothing in you . . . you'll be a man, my son!" Hell, I didn't have anything in me now, and I didn't care if I ever was a man. All I wanted at that point was to lie down and die.

I thought I was beginning to imagine things when I heard the sound of airplane motors, but I wasn't. I grabbed the little radio and lay down on the ground and started calling. An opportunity to rest my weary bones is about all it meant to me; I was so exhausted I'd almost forgotten why I was in this hell. I was so hot, so tired, so wet from sweat it had become a battle just to keep moving.

The cool, firm voice that came out of the set brought me around a little. It was Andy. "Where the hell are you, boy?"

"You've got me," I answered. "But where I am is hell sure enough, though I haven't been introduced to Satan yet."

"Well, get on the ball, Diebold. You haven't got all day, you know."

The injustice of it, I thought. He sits up there in a nice cool cockpit in a blue sky I can barely make out through the foliage, turning a wheel and telling me to get to work.

I counted to ten and then answered him. "Give us four more hours, and I should be with the body, I think."

"Four hours. O.K., we'll be back then, but hurry up."

I was so mad at the absurdity of it that I beat the hot, steaming jungle floor with my fists while the chief, who had come back down the trail to find out what the fuss was about, clucked his disapproval. Andy had only been riding me, but it was tough to take at that point. It was just as well that I didn't speak the chief's language, for I'm certain if I had I would have been in for a fatherly lecture on temperament.

Wearily we ploughed ahead. My throat was raw from the quick gasps of hot air. Somewhere this God-awful churning of the legs and sweat in the eyes must end, I thought.

5

It was unexpected when it happened. Around the corner of some heavy brush, they came into view, the most beautiful sight I'd ever seen—two Naga houses. To me, instead of being surrounded by mud and filth, those two huts seemed made of ice cream and peppermint candy. There's no describing reaching the ultimate goal when everything inside you tells you you'll never make it. It's like a gambler raking in an unbelievable pile of winnings. Home never looked better.

I staggered to the nearest log, slumped down on it, and simply stared at those huts. They were only a hundred yards away, but I didn't think I'd make it even that far. Tomorrow, the day after, a thousand days after that, I didn't think I'd be able to move again.

But when I'd regained my breath I thought better of it and made my way up to the largest of the two huts. On the porch stood a wrinkled old man, a welcoming committee of one. My native friends were standing below the porch looking at the old man, and all were talking at once.

As I approached, the jabbering ceased. I stood with the crowd and looked at the old man, too. "We're in the wrong village again," I moaned. "Not that. I simply can't go any farther." The old man spoke a few words to me, none of which, of course, I could understand, and then he motioned me up on the porch. I climbed the notched log and entered the house after him. As tired as I was, I was getting excited. Was he there?

I peered into the dimly lit front room. Over by the fire I could see the outline of a form stretched out on the floor. I walked over to it, afraid of what I might find, but he was there, lying by the fire, the back of his head toward me. But was he alive?

He twisted around, and I saw his face, and tears were running down his cheeks. Neither of us said a word. I knelt beside him, and we gripped hands. It was impossible to say anything; I was too choked with emotion. I tried an experimental smile, but it was forced, for even though he was alive I thought even now we might be too late. He looked to me as if he were on his way out of this lovely world of ours as he lay there softly sobbing.

He was covered with dirty pieces of cloth, so all I could see of him was his face, but that was enough. It told a horrible story of suffering and starvation and exposure. His beard was long and tangled, his hair spread like a woman's on the log he was using as a pillow. The bones of his cheeks stood out in ugly relief below yellowing, bulging eyes. He spoke, through cracked, fever-ridden lips. "Thank the Almighty. You've come."

I spoke with all the unfelt confidence I could muster. "Right you are, lad, and a couple of doctors will be here in a minute. We'll have you running as good as new in no time and out of this fire trap in a jiffy."

He smiled at my slang, and I realized it must have been a long time since he'd heard any language but Naga. He closed his eyes and gave a long sigh. I was afraid this was it, but then he opened them again. "Have you any food?"

"Coming right up," I answered. "Would some nice warm cereal fit the bill?"

"Of course," he said and closed his eyes. I have never made cereal faster. As I cooked, I could see his hands; they were nothing but bones covered with a layer of skin. He was a human skeleton.

When the food was ready, I fed him. All he was able to take were a few spoonfuls and a couple of sips of tea; he was exhausted from the effort. He seemed to go to sleep or he was in a coma, I couldn't tell. I lifted the dirty burlap the natives had covered him with for an examination. He opened his eyes again when I did this. I hoped my face remained normal when I looked, but my stomach turned inside-out. He was all bones, and his legs and body were covered with huge, ulcerous sores. He was looking at me hard, and I had to say something, so I smiled and said, "Prickly heat, eh?" It was a poor attempt at humor, but he managed a feeble grin.

This boy needed a doctor in the worst way. I began praying for the rescue ship to come. This was too much for my first-aid knowledge of medicine. I replaced the sacking and started talking to him, anything to make him feel better. It seemed to help. As I talked, I could see him improve . . . or at least to become more alert. It made him feel safer. Another American was there, he was rescued.

He told me, in a weak voice, that his name was Greenlaw W. Collins (he actually gave his middle initial) and that he was from New Orleans. I took up the conversation and talked about New Orleans since, luckily, I had been there. He liked to hear me talk of his home, it was easy to see. He mumbled in the middle of one of my sentences that it had been his first Hump trip and his last, he hoped. I assured him he was on his way back to New Orleans as of right now.

"I was flying a pea shooter"—a fighter—"and had engine trouble," he said. "The plane went into a spin, so I had to bail out. I landed in a tree and lost my jungle kit, so I had no food. I followed a river I found. How long I don't know, but it was over three weeks."

Out in this country for more than three weeks without a knife, a compass, food, or anything. This boy was tough, and then some.

"The natives found me going down the river and brought me on a litter up here. Don't know how long that was, I lost track of the days. On the way down that river, I slept on rocks in the middle of the water to get away from the leeches and the animals. My shoes wore out, and the rocks cut my feet to ribbons. It was tough going at times. The natives here have been trying to feed me. It's pretty awful stuff, monkey meat and rice and then rice and monkey meat. I just sorta lost my appetite, I guess."

No wonder, I thought, remembering the smell of burning hair before the meal at the other village. A piece of soot fell from the roof onto his face. He raised a shaking hand and brushed it off.

"Did you get my note?" he asked.

"Yep, that's why I'm here."

"Never thought you would. I thought sure I was a goner. You know, it took me a whole day to write it."

Talking was an effort, and he rested a bit. He closed his eyes, but in a moment he spoke again.

"Didja see those sores on my legs?"

"Yes."

"Well, once they got me here I kept 'em open with a native knife. I thought I had better keep them running. That was right, wasn't it?"

"Perfect. You'll be up and running in a week."

"Thanks," he said with a wry smile. I wasn't fooling him, I could see that.

He told me a little more, and I learned other details later, like his eating bamboo shoots, bitter berries, and even leeches! He talked about the soaking rains, using his socks as gloves and wrapping up his head at night to escape the mosquitoes and crawling pests. In that fetid, humid jungle, his boots rotted and started to fall apart. And most of all he mentioned the cold, how awful cold the nights got, and the terrible, solitary loneliness of that sea of green.

But mostly he seemed to drift in and out of focus. There was no doubt his had been a close thing. What I was worried about was that it was a close thing still, that if we didn't get help there soon, he might not make it.

Then I heard it—the search plane approaching the village. It was faint at first, but in less than a minute it sounded as if the pilot had brought the plane right down in the hut with us. Collins heard it, too, and looked at me.

"Here come your doctors."

I went out on the porch and turned on the radio. Andy's voice came over the ear-phone. "Air rescue calling gravel shuffler. Air rescue calling gravel shuffler."

I was in no mood for jokes right then. "Yeah, this is gravel shuffler, and we need medical help down here as soon as you can get it."

"Stand by Diebold," he answered. "I've got the docs on board, and they'll be right down. How bad is he?"

"He's not too good. Tell them to bring the works as far as equipment goes. And may they be young and strong, for this is no country for the feeble."

"Will do," Andy answered. "And they look pretty big and strong to me."

The plane circled around, and I knew just how those two medicos felt as the big C-47 skimmed down the side of the far mountain. It shot up the side of our mountain and over the village and then a parachute blossomed from the rear. It was exciting to watch from the ground and not a little satisfying. But then the wind caught the falling chute, and it disappeared over the far side of the mountain. I wished the boy luck and then turned to the chief and pointed in the direction the chute had gone. He immediately sent two of his men on the run in that direction.

"Pretty lousy aim," I radioed Andy. "It shouldn't take more than two days to find him out there." He deserved that dig after the gravel shuffler guff he'd been handing me.

Andy didn't answer. Around again came the plane, and the sprawling, tumbling figure of a man flew out of the cargo door of the ship. The figure tumbled and fell straight down, but the chute didn't open. It was free fall, no paratrooper chute! I could see the doctor's arms flailing in the air as his hand grasped for the ripcord and missed. My knees turned to water as I stood there holding my breath. I didn't want to look, but I couldn't tear my eyes away. The sensation of helplessness was awful.

It seemed almost too late when he finally found the ripcord and the chute opened. The canopy streamed out and snapped open above his head, and a split second later he hit the ground. As I ran to where he hit, I hoped and prayed it had opened in time to break his fall. I expected to find him with his hips driven up between his eyebrows. As the natives and I approached on a dead run, he slowly sat up and shook his head.

"My God," he said to no one in particular, "I thought I'd had it."

6

The doc had landed in soft mud at least six inches deep, the chute slowing his fall and the mud cushioning his landing. That was all that saved him from being seriously injured. He was a big man, over six feet with wide, husky shoulders. After I helped him to his feet, he stuck out his hand, and we shook. His fingers were long and narrow but strong. He had a grip like a vise. This must be the surgeon, and did we need him! "My name's Spruell," he said, "although it was damn near mud." We both laughed in relief. "Bill to my friends. I'll look after the patient. You had better try and find our friend. He's somewhere over in that . . ." He waved his hand in the general direction the other chute had fallen.

"The natives have already gone after him," I said. "Don't worry, they'll get him. They've been a big help. Come on, I'll take you to see Lieutenant Collins. He needs you fast, and I'm not foolin'."

Suddenly I remembered the radio. Andy's voice squawked out at me, "Get on the air, gravel shuffler, get on the air, will ya' before I have to bail out and find out what's goin' on."

"Everything's going to be all right, Andy," I said as the major and I walked toward the hut. As I spoke, I saw the figure of a white man with some natives come limping out of the jungle above the village. "Everything *is* all right," I corrected. "Everyone accounted for and unhurt as far as I can tell."

"Whew! I'm sure happy as hell about that. They had me plenty worried."

"Don't think for a minute they weren't worried, too."

"Right," he said. "Is there anything else you want?"

"Better stick around for a few minutes until the doc takes a look at Collins. He may need more supplies than we have here, although I can't see what it'd be except a kitchen sink or something."

"If he wants one, tell him we'll drop it."

Around us the natives had gone wild. This was too much for them, a big noisy airplane swooping over the mountain, men dropping from the skies all over the place.

Inside the hut, the major took a quick look at Collins while I laid out the medical supplies dropped to me the day before. The major rummaged through them. "Tell them all I need is some glycerin."

I told Andy who radioed back, "O.K., I'll be back with it in the morning. Good luck, old top."

Up the notched log came the other parachutist. We

shook hands, and he introduced himself as Captain "Sandy" Morrissey from Milwaukee, Wisconsin.

The two doctors went immediately to work on Collins. I watched them start to give him blood plasma, and though I wanted to help they didn't seem to need me. Then I thought I'd better be paying off the natives who had helped bring the stuff over from the other village; they might want to go home again. I opened the pack I'd carried and took out my bag of silver rupees. I went down the ladder and tried to hand each of the natives a couple, but they wouldn't take them from me. Instead, they pointed to the chief, so I turned to him and gave him a handful. He took them, went around to each of the natives, and handed them one apiece, then he handed the remainder back to me, keeping one himself.

One rupee, about thirty cents American for all that work. I handed the chief back the extra rupees, enough for another round, and motioned that he give them to the others. Everyone looked highly pleased. Sixty cents for all that mountain climbing burdened down with heavy packs, and they considered it high wages. *What a place to retire,* I thought.

But the natives seemed in no hurry to leave. Night was coming on, and, after some discussion with the chief, they decided to stay. Immediately upon a decision being reached, they all tried to move into the front room where the doctors were working on Collins. That just wouldn't do even if their intentions were innocent of everything save, perhaps, curiosity. I started to shoo them out, but that lovely creature, my hand-holder-in-the-stream from earlier in the day, seemed to be more reluctant to leave than the others. Since both the doctors were busy with things I would be of little assistance in, I decided I'd best walk her home. Home, of course, was the other hut fifty yards away. Feeling the way I did, I wouldn't have gone any farther for Hedy Lamarr.

As we slooshed through the mud, hand in hand, we must have made quite a picture. Hands across the sea, as it were, or "make friends with the inhabitants of this strange country, soldier," and I believed in obeying orders. I knew one word of her language, and she knew none of mine. We carried on an interesting conversation; I'd smile, then she would smile. Then I would say "Kajaiee" and she would say "Mmmmmmum," or something like that. Our cultural advancement through association seemed to work fine.

The party in the other hut had started when we got there, and my date and I were invited. I had named her Butch, and she seemed to think that was about perfect. At every mention of it I received a beaming smile. So when we entered the hut I asked her, accompanied by the appropriate gestures, "How about a drink, Butch?"

She replied, "Ummmmm glug glug!" or so it sounded.

"Fine, what kind of rice wine do you prefer? The type without the hulls in it, I suppose, since you're the finer type."

"Apko chinta ummmmmmmum!" she answered. I began to wish I knew what "ummmmmmum" meant. I thought I could guess, though.

Curiously, the Naga seemed to be feeling the same elation I felt, and everyone was talking at once. A white liquid was produced, as well as pipes, which even the women smoked. Butch was the first date I'd ever had who brought out a pipe and started smoking, but then I hadn't been in the States since the cigarette shortage. The white liquid, I correctly guessed, was rice wine. The rice they fermented this stuff from must have been a near relative to the barley family. It was hard stuff. I took a drink and reached for my head, which was lying on the floor or the ceiling or someplace; all I knew was that it wasn't on my shoulders. What a drink! Vodka is like water compared to this stuff.

After a couple of slugs apiece, we all started singing to the accompaniment of a wheezy old flute. My date and I put our heads together, and we could really yodel Naga. Then I resurrected a couple of stanzas of "Old McDonald Had a Farm," a song at least all the natives from the other village were familiar with. I can't sing worth a damn, but neither could these people, so they didn't know the difference. Then the natives from this village, taking the lead from the ones I had sung with the night before, quickly learned to chime in on the E-I-E-I-O. It was a glorious chorus!

In an hour or so, the major came for me, figuring where I was from the racket and the wacky chorus from Old McDonald. He pulled on one hand, and the gal pulled on the other as he tried to drag me away for dinner. *Who in the hell wants to eat at a time like this?* I thought as the major won the tug-of-war. But he didn't want me to eat, he wanted me to cook. I had been elected, it seemed. I got even with those two for that. I whipped them up a luscious meal of Spam and beans from our supplies.

While I had been gone, Major Spruell and Captain Morrissey had given Collins blood plasma, lanced his sores, which I learned were ulcerated, shaved him—thus finding a use for the shaving cream we'd lugged across two mountains—cut his hair, and given him an alcohol rubdown. Then I fed him some more cereal and he fell asleep almost immediately. He was going to be all right, they told me . . . if we could get him out of here. I doubted that when I thought of the miles and miles of jungle between us and any type of civilization. If "getting out" was anything like the trails I had been on today, staying where we were seemed more likely.

After dinner I had a couple of nifty drinks made from lemon powder and rubbing alcohol, and the doctors and I sat down on the floor and talked the whole thing over.

"Lieutenant Collins needs a few days more here," the major said, "so we can bring his strength up before we attempt to move him."

That'll give me a few days to get better acquainted with the villagers, I thought. Love thy neighbor is my motto.

"What are you mumbling about?" Sandy asked.

"Nothing, nothing. Just concurring with the major's ideas."

Later, when some of the natives from the overcrowded adjacent house had joined us in the hospital hut, the evening warmed up—though we suspended our singing to keep things a little quieter for Collins. The firelight twinkled merrily, and the chief and his friends got their pipes gurgling. Opium smoke permeated the air. (The docs decided the pungent smoke wouldn't hurt Collins and might actually help him sleep.) I sat there sipping rubbing alcohol and lemon water feeling very contented as I watched the moon rise through the open door.

My little Naga friend was trying out one of our combs on her long, thick black tresses as Sandy and Bill looked on enviously and made cracks such as, "What does she see in him?" to which I answered, "Love, my friends, is blind. And anyway she knows a man when she sees one." They replied with unjustifiable remarks about my looks or character or whatever happened to strike their medicized brains.

The only thing marring the evening was the thought of that long trek out. It really didn't seem possible we could make it. Not in a couple of weeks or in a couple of months would our man Collins be in shape to walk out on that tortuous trail over mountains and through the jungle. For him, it would be the litter or nothing. For that I sort of envied him.

I had a map of the area and could see the mountain we were on and the big river where we'd taken our first swim. The three of us sat there discussing the pros and cons of the situation. We'd been measuring the number of miles from where we were to the Ledo Road, the nearest place where we could be picked up. As the crow flew, it was roughly fifty miles, but we weren't crows, so we added another fifty miles up and down hills.

As we talked, my eyes were drawn to the river the Naga and I had swum in that morning. It ran a crooked narrow course until it flowed into a larger and straighter river. The larger river's path—the map identified it as the

Tarung River—led straight down to the Ledo Road. It was a way out without walking, but that current had been swift. Could a boat make it?

"I've got it," I said.

"Well, hang onto it," said the surgeon. "I'll examine it in the morning."

"Corn, strictly corn, from way back," I snarled, my enthusiasm only slightly dampened. "But while you two books of knowledge are sitting over there patting each other on the backs and knocking yourselves out with mutual flattery about your parachute jumps, I've been thinking."

"With what?" they asked in unison—fine friends.

"Well, if it were up to you two, we'd walk our tails off, or sit here and rot. That's not for this apple."

"O.K., genius, go ahead. What's your plan?" the major asked.

I pointed to the map. "See that river there? Today I took a bath in it, and—"

"Interesting, very interesting," Sandy interrupted, "but you don't look it."

"Could be the environment," I murmured, shooting him my best glare. "*Anyway*, that river is navigable, if one doesn't mind shooting a few rapids."

"Where would we get the boat if we did want to try it?" Sandy asked.

"Maybe they would drop us one from the plane. A big rubber one, big enough to hold all four of us."

"The guy's crazy," Sandy laughed. "Not enough that

we have to bail out of airplanes, but now he wants us to shoot rapids in a rubber boat."

For all their wisecracking, the idea seemed to interest them, though, and they took a closer look at the map and asked me questions about the river. They'd flown over the same mountains I had, and any alternative, even a wild river, seemed worth considering. After much discussion, we decided to ask the rescue ship the next morning to take a look at the river and, if it looked like it could be navigated, to drop us a boat, if they had one and if they could. A lot of ifs, but it was worth a try.

But that was a decision for tomorrow, and we decided to turn in. That night the animal noises outside the hut didn't bother me. Maybe I was getting used to them, but the mere presence of others to talk to—without having to use sign language—made it all seem real instead of a fantastic dream. There was a hitch to our bedtime, though: We had failed to put up beds.

Sandy and Bill started to rig up their jungle hammocks. This hut had large, thick uprights supporting the roof. To these they attached their hammocks. After last night, I was through with jungle hammocks, so I threw a blanket on the floor near the fire with the chief and his men, then settled back to watch the fun. I expected Sandy and Bill to have the same trouble I had the night before.

I was disappointed. Both of them had been checked out in the proper care and feeding of a jungle hammock, and, just like that, they were all settled and comfortable and laughing down their respective noses at me. Then

Greenie woke up—we were all calling him that now—and was hungry again. Since I was the closest one to him, or something like that, I was elected to get up and cook him some food.

The natives grumbled and objected to this as I stumbled over their sleeping bodies in search of the proper ingredients for making cereal and cream. But given the day we'd had, they were tired enough to go back to sleep. So was I, but getting Greenie strong meant getting him to better health, and food was what he needed.

With my feet in the chief's face, I knelt down and blew on the fire, as I had seen him do, to raise a flame. The sparks from the ashes floated around the room, burning all or any tails they happened to land on. I was most unpopular. Actually I was doing some good. Greenie was laughing at me, and Sandy fell out of his hammock in a fit of hysteria—and I didn't push him more than once.

7

Either the Naga had tougher hides than I did, or generations of flea and mosquito bites had convinced them of their lot, and they'd become insensitive. Word had gotten around to all the mosquitoes in Burma that I was sleeping without a net. Fresh, raw meat, straight from the United States. And did they ever take advantage of it! Not a Naga squirmed throughout the night, but I batted myself silly, slapping my face at every landing. The buzzing in my ears wasn't too bad, but when my face became overcrowded with mosquitoes, something like Coney Island on a hot day, a couple of money-wise mosquitoes started selling reserved space up my nose.

That was what was happening to the part of my body exposed and protruding from under the blanket. Underneath the blanket, the fleas sat around my unprotected body, rubbing their claws together, licking their chops, and, at a given signal, diving into the meat. When I wasn't batting my face into a horrible mess, I was scratching my skin raw. When I scratched, the fleas sat back and waited. When I stopped, they all dived in, chewing lustily. Then Greenie would wake up for another mouthful of cereal: more ashes, more burnt tails, and more muttering by the natives. All in all, it was a rather awful night.

It was a cheerless sight to watch Sandy and Bill wake up, climb out of their clean hammocks, chattering noisily about the wonderful night's sleep they'd had. I put my tail between my legs and took my battered and bleeding body to the nearest stream for a bath. The pigs and dogs, grunting and yelping, followed me down the path.

Early mornings on the tops of mountains are, to say the least, chilly. Mountain streams are in contravention to all facts of science; water that cold should be frozen solid. As is, they're a booby trap to the unsuspecting. I stuck my toe in the water while the pigs looked on, snorting. When I felt the temperature of that water, every nerve in my body demanded I join the pig clan behind me. But the fleas had to go, so in I stepped. From there on, it was a matter of washing around the goosebumps. Not even a healthy flea could live at that temperature.

Later that morning, the search plane flew over and dropped the glycerin. Again, Andy was the pilot, and I told him of our proposed plan for evacuating the patient. Andy sounded doubtful, but he flew over the river for a while and returned to us with a report.

"I don't know, Bill. That river is full of rapids and looks as mean as any body of water I've seen. I don't think your plan is practical."

"Well, Andy," I explained, "it'll be almost an impossibility to drag Collins out through all that jungle. These are narrow trails, and all of them would need to be widened before a litter could pass through. The trip would also be dangerous as the trail hangs onto the vertical sides of the mountains. Then look how hard it would be on Collins, and could he stand the gaff, considering his condition?"

"You may have something there," Andy radioed back. "I'll need to check with Major Hedrick, but he'll probably give the O.K.; you're the man on the ground. I'll drop the rubber boat if you want it, but it's your responsibility."

Two days later Andy dropped us a boat, landing it right in the center of the clearing. It was a good shot; I had been worried the raft might be damaged if it came down in the jungle, but he put it right on the money.

We were far from ready to go, however. For one, we needed to wait a little longer for Greenie to improve. He was a tough kid, and his powers of recuperation were as strong as his will to survive had been. It was, after all, what had kept him alive in the jungle for nearly a month. After my comparably short trek to find him, I had all the respect in the world for what he'd done. But he needed a little more time.

Greenie improved quickly under the constant care of the two doctors, and from all the food I spooned into him. After a week, we figured it to be about time to start the arduous journey down to the river.

By now I was getting used to how quickly the Naga could pick up on an idea, and they were nothing if not resourceful. With a few gestures and pantomimes from me and the two doctors, and with the help of a little diagram we drew, the natives made us a litter. They even improved on our plan. It was solidly built of bamboo, had a woven "bed," and featured very long end poles so it could be carried by no fewer than eight men. We laid Greenie on this and strapped him down. But even our moving him onto the litter caused him a great deal of pain, so one of the medics doped him up pretty well. We had a mountain to descend to get to the river, and this was going to be a rough trip. They made a similar litter for the raft; though uninflated, it was still heavy and took several natives to carry it.

When we were ready to leave, I approached the chief in whose village we had stayed and who had been instrumental in saving Greenie's life. I hadn't the least idea what was or was not of value to him. I gave him a hundred silver rupees, wondering what he would do with them. There was nothing out here I could see to spend them on. Then I gave him a couple of extra G.I. jungle knives we had and some "jewelry" for his wives, all of which had been dropped from the air. The knives seemed to please him most for he beamed and nodded approval. All this I knew would make it even easier going for the next airman who might come down in this section of the country.

Finally, with smiles from our new friends and much shouting and barking of mongrels and waving of hands, we were off down the trail. Naturally, Butch, my constant companion, came along. She looked like she was set to come back to America with me. I could just imagine my wife's face when I brought this cute little number home as my adopted daughter.

The way we took down to the river was different, and, as I'd expected, the trip wasn't easy. In front, two men were constantly cutting trail, widening it for the litter to pass. Though I didn't know it at the time, the future would bring more of these expeditions for me, rescuing airmen, but few of them brought me more willing or harder-working natives. Again and again I realized how impossible this whole expedition would have been without their help.

The trail was steep and, at times, clung to the sheer mountain wall. Lieutenant Collins could look over his litter and see straight down for five hundred feet or so. He didn't look often. The natives carrying him were as sure-footed as mountain goats and never slipped, though sometimes the slope felt like it was more than seventy degrees. Sweat poured down their husky backs as they grunted and heaved the litter along. They swore and muttered in their own language, and they even used a couple of words in English we had taught them. It was a tough trip, but at four o'clock that afternoon, we hit the river. Our total take on the trip was one snake—a pit viper and poisonous as hell—two small barking deer, and an aggressive monkey of sizable proportions.

At the river, we made camp and cooked dinner. The monkey that had briefly annoyed us went to the Naga, as well as one of the deer. The other deer we cut into steaks and roasted on a spit over the fire. It was a delicious dinner. The natives, naturally, cooked the monkey as well as their deer. Out of sheer curiosity, I had to have a taste of the monkey. For the record, may I say that the anatomical resemblance of a monkey, so akin to a human, makes one feel a bit on the cannibalistic side. Apart from that, he didn't taste as bad as I thought he might.

That night we all went fishing in the river. In one pool we had some luck. The pools being places behind rocks where the water slowed down to thirty miles per, we were able to get in a line and catch fish. We called them skin fish, not unlike the American catfish, and they weighed up to five pounds.

Collins had weathered the trip in fine style and was sleeping soundly. After we caught our fish, Sandy, Bill, and I had a fish fry. It was late, but we were excited about tomorrow's river trip and wanted to talk it over. Where we'd camped, the water was a roaring, angry beast with froth on its mouth. Its course twisted down the narrow gorge while the water stormed into the curves with a vengeance, roaring its might as it hit the solid rock embankments. The water was swift and deep, for it had been swollen by the monsoons. We knew that, if the boat capsized, only a good swimmer might make it to shore alive. For Greenie, it would probably be impossible.

Directly below our camp and our proposed launching spot were two mean-looking "S" curves. At each curve in the S, the water poured and pounded against the rocks, then changed course ninety degrees to the next curve, where it whirled and churned its way around that one. It was a formidable sight.

In the moonlight, sitting by the fire, we eyed those curves. Bill suggested we carry both patient and boat downstream below the danger point. This seemed an excellent idea—except the mountain wall jutted up almost vertically from the water. It would be a dangerous trip to carry Greenie down there, perhaps even more dangerous than the boat would be. As we pondered the problem, Sandy summed it up laconically enough: "Either way, it looks like a slip, a swish, and a big gulp of water for us."

The final decision was to tie some parachute shroud lines together, doubling them up, wrap one end around one of the boulders, and tie the other to the boat. In this way we could ease the boat down around the curves—or so we hoped.

In the morning we all donned our life jackets (dropped with the boat), inflated the rubber raft, and loaded Greenie aboard. The raft, though not over-large, was big enough to hold us all with a little extra room for our tied-in gear. Spruell went down to the sharpest curve, the first one, to help ward off the boat. He sat on the rim of the rock with his feet hanging over the side, ready for anything that might happen. Sandy climbed into the boat with Greenie. I twisted the doubled line a couple of times around a boulder, hoping it would act like a brake. Those doubled lines should hold a pull of up to four hundred pounds, we'd figured. We were all set to go!

I gave each of the natives who had helped us down the trail a silver rupee apiece and all the extra equipment we couldn't put in the boat. They were very satisfied, if a little awed at what they saw we were going to try to do. One of them kept holding me by the arm, trying to stop me. It was Butch. She had tears in her eyes and kept pointing to the water and shaking her head. I was tempted, but, if I gave in now, we were sunk, and there was no other way out of this wilderness as far as I could see. The two of us stood there arguing with our eyes and through sign language when Sandy yelled out, "Enough. Let's get goin'."

Turning away, I went over to my position at the rock, and called back, "O.K. boy, let 'er rip!"

Sandy shoved off into the current and jumped into the boat.

Immediately we were in trouble. The boat began to toss and jump on the surface of the boiling water. I played out the line as slowly as I dared, but the strain was terrific and, four hundred pounds or no, the lines snapped and the little raft shot down the current. I held my breath as Sandy gave a yell and the boat shot into the first curve. He was paddling frantically but ineffectually as the bobbing bit of rubber swung around; they were going backward into that pounding torrent of rock and thundering water.

The raft hit the rock wall with terrific force, doubling as one might break a doughnut in two. Its two occupants held on frantically. The boat rebounded from the wall like a rubber ball, hit the current again and shot off, whirling around and spinning into the next curve where the same slam-bang happened again.

Spruell had fallen off the rock trying to ward off the boat and had vanished into the current. I wished him luck but fully expected never to see him again. I was left alone with the natives who were gaping at the place where the boat had disappeared around the curve. I tried to make a hurried march down the side of the stream, first taking the precaution of inflating my life vest, but the rocks were too slippery for me, and naturally I, too, fell into the river and was swept away. I got one good gulp of air before I hit the icy water, and that was the last gasp, it seemed, for ages. The water grabbed me, turning me head-over-heels, whirling me around. I could feel it churning about my body, and then my head hit the rock wall.

When I regained consciousness, I was bobbing along in a fast but straight-away current. The vest had kept my head up and saved my life. Downstream I saw the yellow life raft beached on a small sandbar, Sandy and Bill busily bailing it out. I came bobbing over to the bar and climbed ashore. When they saw me they let out a yell of welcome, for they had thought I was finished . . . as I had thought they were. We were a rather beaten-up trio—and this was just the beginning of our trip.

After a short rest, we pushed the boat into the swift water again. This time we all climbed aboard. Greenie was in the bottom of the boat, and the three of us perched on the doughnut-like sides with paddles in our hands. Once Greenie stuck his head up over the side and took a look at what was before us. All he could see was foaming rapids with large boulders jutting up over the surface of the water.

"Good heavens," he said. "I'd rather bail out over the Hump anytime than take another trip like this one."

Solemnly and silently we all agreed.

The boat, lacking any type of keel, first went forward, then sideways, and then backward. We paddled, but it did little good. We sailed into a whirlpool and just sat there going around and around. The center of the pool sucked us down, but the buoyancy of the raft kept us afloat. It was like riding a revolving turntable. The pull of gravity had the three of us on the outside hanging on with all our strength. Then the whirlpool, in some fluke of hydraulics, released its hold, and we went sliding across the surface of the water at a terrific clip. Somebody yelled, "Look out!" and, *crash*, we ploughed into a rock jutting up from the current. Why the boat didn't puncture and sink was beyond all realm of reasoning. It bounced off rocks like a rubber ball, spun around, and shot downstream again while we sat there, dazed and unbelieving, hanging on and working our paddles as we could, but in the grip of something far beyond our ability to control or escape.

"Good Lord, look what's ahead of us!" Sandy shouted over the roar of the water.

Ahead of us was a waterfall.

Our luck has been too damn good, I thought as I watched us approach it. This is the end of the line.

The water frothed and boiled over the line of rock and we swept, right into the center of it. The boat shot out and over the waterfall, which was about two feet high. For just a second we were suspended in the air like ski jumpers, and then the boat fell to the water with a sickening thud; in the swirling cauldron of water the raft completely filled and we were sinking.

Overhead a tree limb branched out above the river. Sandy screamed at me, "*Grab that limb!*" I caught hold. I was all but yanked from the boat but somehow managed to hang on to both of them. The drag swung the boat around to the bank, where we beached it, just in time.

We were stopped, and for the moment safe, but we were all cold and wet-through, and poor Greenie was frozen. The sun was out, but it was too early to give us much heat. Quickly tying up the boat, Sandy and I gathered dried bamboo and built a roaring fire and, retrieving supplies from one of our tied-in bags, made some hot coffee. We all sat there, huddled around the fire, a soaked, miserable group, but happy to be alive.

"Well," Sandy said, "we only have a couple of hundred more miles to go."

What a sense of humor, I thought as we sat there toasting first one side and then the other.

Our gloom was dispelled, though, when in the distance we heard the sound of a plane. It flew into sight, and I made a grab for the radio, but the radio was finished: too much water. Luckily, the plane spotted our fire and yellow raft on the riverbank and circled us. The pilot was trying to make radio contact. After five minutes of circling, he realized our radio was out, and we saw the rear door of the Doug come off and the figure of a man appear. He flashed out a code with a signal light, or biscuit gun as the Air Corps calls them. It was good news. As I slowly read the letters and the letters became words, the uplift in our morale was something to write home about.

The flashing light told us that not five miles ahead was the junction of our river and the larger one, the Tarung. Our Search and Rescue Squadron, efficient as ever, had motorboats waiting there for us. We shouted and cheered at the news. Prior to this good word, we'd pictured at least several nights sleeping wet and cold on the riverbank and hazardous days shooting rapids.

Immediately we started out again, our spirits a great deal lighter. The boat still bounced and whirled, but now we laughed instead of holding our breath—help and the end were near. Less than three quarters of an hour later, we shot around a curve in our river, and there was the junction.

Three boats, big landing barges with outboard motors, were waiting for us. The current almost swept us past them, but by paddling frantically we got our boat over to their sandbar.

Cameras flashed (Public Relations always in there pitching), hot coffee was ready, and there was good dry clothing. Our rescuers were M. K. O'Heeran of Houston, Texas, who acted like he did this sort of thing every day, and Lt. Glenn Dateman from East Cleveland, Ohio. Those two men were certainly a sight for our sore eyes.

Evidently Major Hedrick, not having total confidence in my newfound abilities in jungle navigation, had also launched a ground rescue a few days after my jump. Or rather, a water rescue. At first the team had thought they might be able to travel up the Tarung from the Ledo Road and then force their motorboats up the river we'd just descended and from there somehow get to the mountain top. But our river, smaller and faster than the Tarung, had defeated their barges. By that time, we'd come up with the idea of a raft, and they decided to wait for us to come to them. Whatever had put them there, though, we were sure glad to see them.

After we lifted Greenie out of the raft, Major Spruell put new dressings on his ulcers. We put clean clothing on him, about four sizes too large; we later learned he had lost 55 of his normal 165 pounds. With that thin face and those outsized clothes, he really made a ludicrous picture. Into one of the barges we loaded the rubber raft, which we planned to save as a souvenir, and laid Greenie on it. It made a perfect air mattress when turned upside down. The remainder of the trip was easy. Although this river, too, was full of rapids, the big boats chugged along with ease. We rode all the rest of the day, and that night brought us to the comparative comfort of semi-civilization on the Ledo Road. Search and Rescue had an ambulance waiting.

Greenie was soon loaded in and ready to head off to a nearby hospital. When we lifted him into the ambulance, he stuck out his hand and said, "Thanks is a small word to use when you've saved my life, but . . . Aw, hell! Thanks a lot for everything." It wasn't much of a speech as speeches go, but it was all we wanted, for we knew it was sincere. That boy Collins was all right for our money, we all agreed.

The next day at a nearby airfield, a Search and Rescue Doug picked up me and the two doctors, and we were off to Assam, India, and home.

In Assam we all shook hands and said the usual farewells, but it was easy to see we hated to part, the two Docs and I. The trip, so full of dangers, had drawn us closer together than anything else ever could. There was a big job to be done pulling these pilots out of the jungle for men who liked the work.

I, for one, had decided I did.

8

The basha was the same, Major Hedrick was the same shrewd personality, still puffing on the stub of a cigar, and all the Hump pilots were accounted for. Things settled down to a routine as I made out the official reports of the trip. It was a respite I was grateful for; after all, I had been on the base for less than a day before flying off over the jungle and jumping from an airplane.

My bunkmate Charlie King waived the "investment" on the basha's furniture. I met a few of the other squadron members and found a little time to have a drink or two with Andy, my search pilot. I also began to study some of the maps Major Hedrick had on his wall and learned a little about how the outfit worked. It was all very peaceful—and I wasn't doing the cooking.

But it didn't last long.

A few mornings after my return to the unit, one of our search pilots reported seeing panels in a village. The village was in the center of a valley in northern Burma. When the pilot of the search ship had first spotted the panels he'd dropped a streamer with a note inside asking, "If there's an American in trouble in the village, put out a large 'X.'" Shortly after, some natives scurried about, and a large white X appeared. The pilot flew back for me, and, after a briefing from Major Hedrick, I readied myself for a jump.

This time there would be no paratrooper chute; we had used them all in the Collins rescue. An ordinary seat-pack chute, drawn from among hundreds, would be the one I used. I didn't feel too good about this. A paratrooper chute is automatically opened by a line attached to the plane and is almost infallible. A seat pack has a ripcord that must be pulled by the wearer before the thing will open. I remembered Spruell's tumbling jump into the Collins village, and that didn't help my morale much.

We took off in the plane for the village. As I sat in the rear of the Doug and watched the ground drop away, I had much the same feeling I'd had the last time. Things weren't improving with age. Soon, sooner than I liked, we were flying over a broad Burma valley and approaching the village. It consisted of a small hole in the jungle with a couple of long huts in it. Running along beside it was a river. *Not again. Not that.*

We circled the village a few times, and the pilot, Lt. Dee McCreary from Commerce, Texas, which he always called the "Cow-town," identified it as the village where the panels had appeared.

Lt. Homer LeClaire of Haskell, Texas, the co-pilot, said, "Let's go down and give 'er the old buzz job and see what we stir up." And down we went!

Those two Texas boys really did it up brown. Th[e]
buzz job was impressive. After a couple of passes in wh[ich]
we very nearly lifted the roofs from the huts, a w[hite]
banner was raised on a long pole. At the time I rem[em]-
ber wondering if it was a surrender flag or a signal. [I]
dropped them another streamer with a note: "If there i[s an]
American there who needs help, take down the flag." [I]
knew these people couldn't read or write English, so i[f the]
flag came down there had to be an American somew[here]
on the premises. Naturally we wondered why he d[idn't]
come out and signal or something, anything, but the[n fig]-
ured that perhaps, like Collins, he was too sick to be [able]
to make it.

The flag came down. "There it goes, Bill." McC[rary]
said. "You all set to go?"

I don't think I was ever less set to go anywhere[, but]
what the hell. "Sure," I answered. "Just ring the bell[and]
I'll see what's going on down there."

Maybe a trifle braver than the last time I had jum[ped,]
I stuck my head into the roaring slip-stream as I sto[od in]
the open door. Spread out below me lay the wide ex[panse]
of valley. There were miles and yet more miles of tr[ees,]
green. It would have looked inviting if I hadn't a[lready]
picked up the knowledge of how dense it really was. [There]
are few natural things a man can eat down there, an[d pen]-
etrating the tangled underbrush is almost an imposs[ibility]
when not on an old, established trail. If Dee missed [drop]-
ping me in that little hole in the jungle, it would pr[obably]
take me forever to make my way back to the village[. Then]
there was always the chance of being ripped apart [by]

limbs. I even thought of such absurd things as landing on a cobra or viper. Then the bell rang!

I fell for a second or two before I remembered that this time there was a ripcord to pull. So far it didn't seem as if I were falling at all. I reached over with my right hand and took hold of the iron ring and gave it a yank. It came out easily, and, remembering from somewhere that the ring was supposed to be saved as a proof that you weren't frightened, I immediately threw it away.

After a short pause I heard the rustle of silk behind me and felt a slight jerk as the canopy spread out above me—what a glorious sight. It seemed all very comfortable this time and my heart sang . . . until I looked down, and then it sank. The village was at least a half mile away from me; Dee had missed the mark. Quickly I took out my compass and shot a bearing on the village, not easy to do in a swinging parachute. If I landed O.K., I had to know in what direction to cut.

Luck was with me, and I barely missed a tall, dangerous-looking tree. I'd been heading right for it, but by pulling the shroud lines until I was almost chinning myself on them, I tipped the chute past it. My slipping, though, had increased the rate of fall, and I landed in a thorn bush with a terrific jar. The thorns on the bush were an inch long. I was pretty well cut up and bleeding but not seriously.

With my knife, I had to whittle room to swing my arms before I could start any real cutting; the jungle was that thick. This, even before I could get out of my chute harness.

It took a full minute of cutting with a machete to get out of the thorn bush and walk a single step. What a

country! Dee in the Doug buzzed my white chute in the brush a couple of times. I couldn't see him through the tangled overhead, nor could I make any sort of signal that I was still ticking and in one piece. Finally, as I continued cutting, I could hear the lazy drone as he contented himself circling the village. He was waiting and hoping I would soon appear. His circling was a help, for it gave me, in general, the direction of the village. In the hope the natives in the village had started out to find me, I continuously called out my one Burmese word, "Kajaiee." It was the only word I knew, and I hoped they knew it, too. Anyway, the noise of my shouting might help them locate me.

Sure enough, after about half an hour of hacking I met the Kachins, another Burma tribe that my pre-flight briefing had indicated lived in this area of the country. They called to me through the bush, and when we finally got together they smiled and actually shook hands. The British had once controlled this valley, and the Kachins were more or less accustomed to the ways of the English and Americans.

Along the trail they'd cut, a lot wider than mine, they led me back to their village. It was larger than I had expected. Like in the Naga village, there were the same two houses, but they were two hundred feet long. On the edge of the jungle were a couple of smaller sheds we hadn't been able to see from the air. When we entered the cleared area around the house, I immediately laid out my parachute (the natives had retrieved it, no doubt hoping I'd give them the valuable silk), and Dee and Homer came down for a look. They came so low that not only could they see it was me standing there, they could count the fillings in my teeth as I stared open-mouthed at the plane. Then they started dropping the supplies.

As the parachutes floated down, I questioned the old man who had come along with the party of young bucks to find me. He was being given the usual deferential attentions due to the head man, so I took it he was the chief of the village. When he didn't respond to my questions, it became the old pantomime between us, more or less the same sign language I'd used with the Naga. When I pointed to his house and asked "American?" he shook his head. Again my heart fell, but rose when he pointed off to the north at some mountains and said "American." Then I laid my head on my hands, closed my eyes and pretended to be sleeping as I held up one finger. Again he shook his head in the negative but seemed to have grasped the idea admirably, for he laid his head on his hands, closed his eyes and held up three fingers. He meant, I took it, that there was an American three sleeps to the north.

In the meantime, Dee had dropped the three packs directly into the clearing, making up a little for having missed when he dropped me. It didn't make me feel any better, but it probably lifted his morale considerably. I fished the little radio from one of the packs and started calling the plane. They were calling me, too, but evidently weren't receiving me. I cut one of the dropped chutes into strips and paneled out: AMERICAN 3 DAYS NORTH—RECEIVING YOU—TRANSMIT NOT WORKING.

Dee got on the air then and asked if I was going and, if so, when I would start. I paneled: YES—TOMORROW.

Then my little radio gave a squawk and died alto-gether. The last I heard was "good luck."

I turned to the natives. I wanted to find out who knew English. Someone must have been able to read our notes. I tried in every way I knew to find out who or how they had known to raise and lower the flag and all the other things they'd done but met with no success. Either the old chief didn't know what I meant or he was keeping his secret a secret. It was just one of those things that belong to the fathomless, mysterious background of the people who live in Burma.

The Kachin were small, light-brown people, slight but well built. Their Mongolian eye-fold was barely percep-tible in some, while in others there was a marked Oriental or Mongolian resemblance. I found some of the Kachin lovely, but in the majority they were not. On the other hand, these people seemed far cleaner than the Naga up in the hills. Some of that impression might have had to do with their clothing: Fighting had taken place in this area between the Japanese and the Allies, and some of them wore pieces of American, Chinese, and British uniforms. Some wore cloth around their bodies, held on with a belt of cord. There were short skirts on the men and long ones on the women. And, like the Naga, some had their hair piled on top of their heads while others had it cut in a short bob. It was a peculiar mixture of Occidental and age-old custom.

These people, I knew, had been a great help to the Allies in the fight against Japan. They hated the Japs about as much as any people I've ever had the pleasure to meet.

As I began to know them better, they told me stories of rape and cruelty that curled my hair. Entire villages had been burned to the ground; babies had been butchered; women fled to the hills, and the men joined the Allies. As jungle troops, I knew, they were unsurpassable. Now the Japs had moved south, and the men and women were returning to their homes. They had to start from scratch, though, for the Japs had taken all of their livestock and burnt their grain. They were a miserable, wretched people but with an indomitable will and, as I learned, a sense of humor. I liked them and hoped to win their friendship.

That night I gave them a large bag of rice that had been dropped from the plane, but, to avoid starting another cooking spree as had happened with the Naga, I decided to eat their food with them. The dinner consisted of dried meat, the origin of which I was unable to determine, and, of course, rice. It was a passable meal and had the added advantage that I hadn't had to cook it.

In its layout and construction—apart from the larger-sized huts—this village was about the same as the Naga villages I'd been in. There was the usual "mud" around the huts, the too few chickens and pigs and, of course, the mongrel, sad-eyed dogs. Their houses were so long, I found out, because they housed a number of families. Each lived in a separate room or compartment, partitioned off from each other by bamboo. Each one of these compartments had its own fire. I could never figure why these buildings with their grass roofs and no chimneys didn't burn down.

In the front of the house, near the usual porch, was the largest room of all. The fire here was surrounded by short logs, which the natives used as pillows while smoking opium. Not all of these natives smoked opium, but most of the older ones did—a privilege of age perhaps. On their walls were skulls of cattle and deer, but I could see nothing that intimated there might be a human head around. In several ways, the Kachin seemed less fierce and more familiar with Western ways than the Naga.

After we had eaten dinner from a large green leaf, the natives commenced to smoke, some cigarettes, some opium, and at the same time offered me the best they had in the house, rice beer. (Curiously, at no time in Burma did any natives offer me a pipe-full of opium. Perhaps they thought that since I had cigarettes I'd ask for a pipe if I wanted one.) Rice beer, unlike rice wine, has little or no kick to it, nor is it invigorating. It merely tastes good and is a nice soft drink. During a lull in the "conversation," conducted largely through the usual pantomime, I tried to find out more about the American from the chief, but either he knew no more or wasn't to be troubled during his smoking. I couldn't tell. All I know is he told me nothing.

Sleep that night was nearly impossible. In the first place, the mosquitoes were fierce. In the second place, a baby wailed continuously from one of the back rooms. Being a father myself and having heard the wail of a baby on many a night, I figured this was a hungry child. So rather than spend the night awake, I got up to see if walking the baby would help. But of course I made a disturbance: As I tramped down the narrow corridor to the back of the hut, the entire household woke up, and grumbling and murmuring emerged from the compartments as I passed. Being a great deal heavier than these little people, my tread caused the floor to shake, waking them all up—as if they could be asleep with the crying going on.

The baby I found in the arms of her father, or I presumed he was the father; no women were in the compartment. The old chief, who I had probably awakened, came in behind me and, through sign language, explained the baby's mother had died a couple of days before. The child was still in the suckling stage, and, naturally, there was no such thing as a baby bottle with a nipple for them to use, so I guessed the baby hadn't been fed since her mother died. No wonder she was wailing.

I went back to my pack and got some canned milk and a D ration bar, which is highly concentrated chocolate. I warmed the milk over the still glowing coals of the evening's fire and scraped a few shreds of chocolate into it. By now, everyone in the house was up and standing around watching what I was doing. Evidently they'd been kept awake several nights, at least partly, by this baby's yells—at least two nights anyway and maybe more—while the mother was ill. They were obviously hoping for the best.

When I got my scratch "formula" warm, I took the baby from the man and held her on my lap. She was a tiny thing and skinny as a skeleton; how she had lived this long was a mystery to me. With an eyedropper I'd pulled from the medical kit, I squeezed a few drops of the chocolate milk into her mouth, then a few more. Immediately she stopped crying and swallowed drops as fast as I could feed her. I was afraid, though, to give her too much, so after a couple thimblefuls I stopped. I held her for a while as I remembered holding my own daughter, and soon she fell asleep. I tried to hand her sleeping little body back to her father, but he would have none of it. He shook his head vigorously, pointed at me, and refused to take her. I had just inherited a baby.

I took her back to my bed and laid her beside me. Every time she woke I warmed more milk, every hour through the night. I was hoping to give her back to her dad in the morning, but, no, she was all mine as far as he was concerned. He held her and carried her, but the minute she started crying he handed her back to me. We were like a couple of old maids with that child, and as time went on I found myself really beginning to grow fond of her. She had an appalling appetite, though.

That morning I held sick call for the natives and dressed their usual jungle sores with sulfa drugs; word had gotten around about my care of the baby, and they were lined up almost before I got out of the sack. Finally, around nine in the morning we started our trek, and, of course, the father and "our" child were part of the procession.

On the trail we had to stop from time to time so I could feed the baby—again and again. All of this necessitated building a fire at each stop so we didn't make good time. It was the damnedest jungle caravan. At least the chief assured me we were headed in the right direction, but what an odd rescue party we were.

In the afternoon we came to a broad, fast river. Without a thought, the natives plunged right into it and started walking upstream against the swift current over slippery rocks. As we stumbled along, I wondered what the hell the native in front of me was doing; he was swinging his knife back and forth in the water. I thought he might be practicing his golf strokes or maybe he was just leaving his mark on the stream. All in all, I was puzzled.

But his actions became clear when we left the stream an hour later. Glancing at the native behind me, I did a quick double take, for the character had a basket full of fish. They had all been nicked with a knife cut. The native in front of me had been nicking and stabbing them with his knife, and the bird behind me had been picking the wounded fish out of the water. It was almost unbelievable, except I was looking at a basket of fish. That night we had rice and the fish for dinner.

The country we were working our way into was apparently uninhabited, and we didn't stay in a village that night. Normally the natives headed for the nearest village when darkness came, but this night we slept on the trail. The track we'd been following was a makeshift sort of thing. During the day we'd walked in the water, following small streams and rivers, but they knew where they were going, I guess, because around four o'clock the natives found a clearing on the edge of one of the streams and started to make camp. I almost fell to my knees in thanks. Walking on the trail was tough, but spending the day pushing against the water and sliding over slippery rocks really finished me.

My new friends were most clever in their jungle lore, and I'm convinced that with bamboo the natives of Burma can do anything. I watched them as they drove high stakes in the ground and over these built a platform, tying everything together with vines from the trees. Over their platform they built a higher, slanting framework and then covered the whole thing with huge leaves cut from the jungle, thus shingling it and making it waterproof. And they could build one of these shelters in a matter of minutes!

During the monsoons in Burma it always rains at night, if not all day, and this was their solution to keeping dry in downpours. Here they quickly erected a little circle of rainproof huts, and in the center of the circle they built a fire. And for everything they used bamboo, some stalks of it as thick as your arm. They cooked in it, drank from it, and used it to carry water from the river to our camp. For that matter, they even used lengths of bamboo as canteens.

Once the fire was going, they built a spit over it and laid a series of bamboo tubes on the spit, the ends over the flames. Rice was then rolled in a large leaf and inserted into the bamboo with water—apparently we were going to have baked rice for dinner. In another tube of bamboo, little red peppers they'd picked along the trail were thrown in together with water and fish. Nor did they bother to clean the fish, simply putting them in the tube as they were, heads, fins, and all. The broth from this boiling mess was a highly seasoned fish soup and not too bad on the taste. It was, though, the first time I'd eaten fish with eyes staring back at me as I took a bite. But after a long hard jungle walk, you can eat almost anything, even something that's looking at you.

As we ate around the fire, a half-dozen bronzed natives and myself, all eating out of large green leaves with our fingers, I thought how unreal and far away the States were. Old Uncle Sugar was in another world as far as I could see, and my own family was impossibly distant. Bouncing the slobbering, happy baby on my knee only added to the incongruity. Curiously, sitting around the fire with my Kachin friends, I was as content as an American from Pennsylvania could be in the jungle. That night the baby and I slept well together.

In the morning we were off again. Soon, though, we left the streams we'd been following and began to climb a mountain. Once we were out of the water it was back to the crawling, sucking leeches. The stinking jungle was as hot and humid as usual, and the trail that day felt long. That night we camped in much the same type of spot we'd camped the night before, with the same rapidly built huts for shelter. There was a difference, though. The chief told me we were near the place where our missing airman should be. How he knew all this was, and still is, a mystery to me. They seemed never to be lost in this impenetrable jungle, and they didn't use drums for signaling (I'd seen that in a movie once), or if they did I couldn't hear them. Yet they always seemed to know where they were and what was going on all over the country.

For two days we climbed that mountain. On the afternoon of the third day we were nearing the summit. On the top of this mountain, the chief had me understand, we would find our American.

9

The last day's march had been the longest yet. The trip had turned into four days, and I was eager to arrive. My native guides had fallen into the spirit of the thing and seemed to know what I was trying to accomplish. Over and over they talked about my dropping from the skies, out of what they called the voom-dit-dit. A very picturesque speech, theirs: Most of the planes they'd ever seen, prior to the one that dropped me, seemed either to be strafing or dropping bombs. The exploding bombs, I took it, accounted for the voom in the word, and the rattle of machine guns accounted for the dit-dit.

After too long a time, we reached the top of our mountain. Around a curve in the trail, I saw an open area, a clearing of felled trees. But what I saw next was hard to believe.

On the far side of the clearing, perched on a log, was a khaki-clad figure. He was simply sitting there, his chin on his fist, watching us approach. He didn't move a muscle or call out, which I thought peculiar for a man being rescued. As we neared him and I could see him better through the sweat in my eyes, I thought he looked in pretty fair shape. Of course he had a beard, but his clothes weren't ripped or dirty, and he seemed well-fed and fat enough. When we were almost up to him, he stirred a little and said, "Well, it's about time you showed up!" That really stopped me in my tracks.

I had heard stories about how men had lost their minds out in the jungle and immediately diagnosed his case as insanity, so I tried to humor him with, "I'm sorry I'm late, but the bus was crowded this morning."

He looked at me quizzically. "Come on, wise guy, where's the rest of 'em?"

He really is in a bad state, I thought. *I wonder how the hell I'll get him out of here? I hope I don't have to tie him and lug the load on my back.*

"Well," I answered, getting nearer to him by degrees, "there are no more men with me, but you'll be all right. Are you hungry, old man?"

"Hungry? Hell, no," and glancing at his watch, "it ain't dinner time yet."

"Take it easy now. A little coffee will make you feel better."

"But I don't want any coffee, and if I did I'd go up to the kitchen and get the cook to give me some."

I began to waver a little. Who was crazy around here, him or me? I thought I'd better try a different tack so I said, "I'm Diebold of the A.T.C. Search and Rescue Squadron.

I've been traveling under the mistaken theory that there was someone up here who needed help."

"Good Lord," he said, raising and offering his hand. "I thought you were part of our relief that's due about now."

I shook the hand, mumbling, "I must be crazy or something, but relief from what?"

"No," he laughed, "you're not nuts. Come on up to the hut and have a cold beer. You've walked into an air raid warning station."

I could hardly believe it; this was the American the chief had heard about. But there were others, too: At the shack was a gang of boys, all healthy and happy. We had a beer or two or three and talked. They tuned in their radio, and we listened to State-side music. Way out here at the end of the earth, I had walked into a little hunk of the U.S.A. At least they were glad to have me around to talk to, for I was the first new man they'd seen in nearly two months. With the radio, they knew more of the current news than I did. What they really wanted was somebody new who hadn't heard all their stories and jokes to sit there and listen. They sat on top of this mountain, on the alert night and day, telegraphing distant points whenever a plane flew over, getting weekly re-supply drops from the air. Rescue, phooey!

That night they killed a couple of suckling pigs, and we had better chow than I would have been given back at the base in Assam. Most of their rations were dropped in the clearing where I had first seen my man. Using their wireless, I sent a radio message to Major Hedrick telling him the mission had been unsuccessful. I got quite a kick out of thinking about the look on his face when he received that wire. As far as he knew, I was deep in the heart of the jungle out of contact with anything civilized, let alone a Western Union station.

The next day, after a good night's sleep on a mattress by the baby, I began thinking of what came next and how I was going to get home. In the meantime, though, I took a hell of a razzing from that bunch of Americans when I fussed with the baby.

"Doesn't look much like her father, does she?" one of them asked another as I neatly changed a parachute-cloth diaper.

"No," he answered, "she's just a little brown, but then maybe Diebold has been out here a long time and can't tell the difference anymore."

They stood around guffawing as I fed her with my eye-dropper. It was all good-natured fun, and the baby didn't seem to mind too much; she just gooed and slobbered a little more.

After a look at the map, a little information from the Americans and the usual "discussion" with my Kachin friends (who were sticking with me), we were off. Now, though, we carried a load of letters these men had written but couldn't mail. At least we were doing something constructive.

It took us a week of steady walking to make it back to a different section of the Ledo Road. During the days after we were off the mountain, we walked mostly through dense jungle or rice paddies. The water in the rice paddies, if you can call it water, is hot and smelly. It was mud to the ankles and hot water to the knees most of the time. For a week my boots were never dry, and I was developing a bang-up case of trench foot. Blisters were rampant. Getting out was a tough trip, and the best that can be said for it is that the baby developed a nice potbelly.

I was also grateful to the natives; they stayed with me the whole way, which was fortunate, for I would have had trouble making that walk on my own. Again, I was struck by the generosity of these "primitive" people. Not only had they helped me find my way through the jungle, they still had a week or more of walking ahead of them to get back to their homes!

When we arrived at the road, the baby's father tried to give her to me. I don't know if he thought raising a baby was beyond him or if he figured I might provide her with a better home, but for a while we stood there, passing her back and forth. I felt pretty silly standing on the edge of a dirt road with trucks roaring by going down to combat with the Japanese, handing a baby back and forth. I almost took her even then, but I already had one back in the States, so I thought he had better keep his offspring. By this time, her dad was pretty adept at feeding her with the eyedropper and mixing the formula. I promised him that a voom-dit-dit would fly over his village every now and then and drop him more milk and D ration. Search and Rescue kept that promise for me. They called it the milk run.

I paid each of them a rupee a day, plus a little baksheesh, which means tip or something. Then I said good-bye—harder than I had thought it might be—took out my thumb, waved it at the first truck that went by, and was given a ride. The truck happened to be part of a Chinese convoy returning men from forward combat areas. The occupants of the truck I hopped into were immediately suspicious of me because of the way I looked, I guess. A Chinese lieutenant asked me what I was. I told him American. He asked to see my dog tags or identification card. Unfortunately, since I didn't need much I.D. in the jungle, I had neither.

As he talked this over with his comrades, I could see he was about to put me under armed arrest as a suspicious character. Then I had a bright idea. I pulled my parachute from my pack and held it up for him to see. I had used part of it as signal panels (and diapers) but had dragged the chute along throughout the entire trip. He immediately got the idea I had hoped he would: that I was a downed pilot. Considering the position I was in, it looked to me to be the only solution. We arrived at a Chinese camp, and he treated me to a sumptuous Chinese dinner—one warrior to another sort of thing. It was a comity I didn't deserve, and it left me a little embarrassed, but with no alternative but to accept.

The next day I was given another ride farther up the road to an American airstrip. Here I was able to hitch a ride over to India by plane. When I arrived there, I got onto the road again and was given another ride back to the base.

It had been an interesting trip—but fruitless.

10

It was good to get back to the basha. Even though I had spent only four or five nights there since arriving in India more than a month ago, it was as close to anything I could call home short of the States. For the first time since I'd been assigned to the place, I had a chance to meet most of the fellows I was supposed to be living with. Many of them were A.T.C. Hump pilots and a damn good gang, and, though they didn't talk about it much, they had one rough job flying supplies over the mountains to China in some of the world's lousiest weather. Most of them had thirty or forty missions over the mountains. But adding everything together, I think they were the craziest bunch of men ever assembled under one roof. One proof of that came almost immediately: That night when I hit the sack, my bed crashed to the floor.

"Don't look at me for that," Charlie King said as I looked accusingly at him. "That's the work of some of our practical jokers." So I was introduced to the basha bunch

—by a completely dilapidated bed. They'd cut the legs on the bed so it would crash at first contact. To this day, I blame Captain "Irish" Riley of Nordham, Texas, but he'd deny it. A week later I repaid him and with a vengeance.

It happened something like this: They had a little bar at the base with very little to drink, but once a month we all were given a case of beer. Some of us spread it over the month, drinking one hot beer a day, while others preferred to knock off the whole case at one sitting. One night, Lt. Herman Furman and I were standing at the bar, and we saw old "Irish" Riley and Captain Anthony Bally of Utica, New York, knocking off their respective monthly rations. This seemed the perfect night to get even with Irish for the chopped bed legs. So Herman Furman, Captain Art Vetter of Brooklyn, New York, and I proceeded to lay our plans.

In the back of the club was a goose pen. Yes, a goose pen—Christmas was nearing, and the mess officer had been picking geese up here and there for months. He was trying to accumulate enough of them for a decent Christmas dinner. Herman, Art, and I selected the largest, meanest-looking bird in the bunch and caught him. Hiding him in a large bag, we carried him over to our basha. Now, each bed in the basha is covered with a mosquito net, and under Riley's we inserted the goose. The goose angrily stomped the length of the bed, finally settling down on Riley's pillow. The Club Bar closed in a few minutes, and we were expecting old Irish soon. We all took various seats and sat back expectantly.

Irish came in feeling pretty good after his case of beer. We could see him vaguely from the moonlight that filtered in through the window. He went over to his bed and sat down on the edge of it to take off his shoes. With a tremendous HONK, the goose flew at the back of Riley's head. Riley gave a scream and landed on the floor. Feathers flew, and the sounds of scuffling and grunting combined with HONKS from the goose woke the whole basha and put us all in a semi-hysterical condition. We almost felt sorry for Irish when the fight was over and he crawled into bed. As he lowered his head onto his pillow, he found that our goose, like all good geese, had to "go" now and then, and Riley's pillow was the spot it had chosen.

A few days later, I was given my next alert. It was the usual setup. Our search ship, piloted this time by Captain Bill Davis of Pampa, Texas, had spotted panels in a village. As a matter of fact, he'd spotted panels in two villages at the same time. These two villages were only about five miles apart, as the crow flies. It was high, rugged mountain terrain in the Naga country again. It was a different area, though, than the one our Lieutenant Collins had gone down in.

Bill Davis and I flew out to take a look, dropping streamers into both villages with notes attached. After our last "rescue" we were wary, so we asked, "If you are an air crew member, put out in panels your ship number." In the smaller of the two villages, a number appeared. It was the number of a ship reported missing in flight. In the other village, on the other hand, nothing changed. They had put out a large "X" with an arrow alongside it, and upon receipt of our note they didn't change it.

There had been a great deal of fighting going on in this territory in the past, and the troops had been supplied by air drops. Our guess, which turned out to be correct, was the natives had become smart and were imitating the panels used by the fighting troops, perhaps explaining the X from the previous mission. They hoped they would be dropped to, by mistake. Sometimes it worked, I imagine, but not this time. When they didn't change their panels, we smelled a rat in the woodpile and ignored them, concentrating on the other village.

After the ship's number appeared and disappeared, a large "RO" was paneled out. We took this to mean he was the radio operator. If he was in that village, then the remainder of the crew was likely to be nearby. Major Hedrick had told me it would be my call, so I decided to jump and look for them. Also, I could help this boy back. He was a hell of a long way from even semi-civilization, and to get to that he would have to pass through an area in which thousands of Naga headhunters lived. As my earlier experience had proven, the Naga were friendly and helpful, but periodic tribal wars bloomed now and again, and when that happened it wasn't too secure for anyone. He also had at least a hundred-mile hike ahead of him, and two of us would be better than one on a rough deal like that. I also hoped to send out native searching parties to round up the remainder of the crew, if they were still alive.

It was worth the attempt, so I climbed into another seat-pack parachute. Lovingly I felt the cold steel of the ripcord handle. "Be a good girl," I whispered to it, "and don't stick when daddy needs you." Then I went forward to the cockpit.

The village where our radio operator had signaled couldn't have been in a worse position. In relation to the surrounding hills, it was situated so the plane could fly over it only when in a steep bank to the right. This made it impossible for me to throw myself out of the door of the Doug because the door was on the left side of the fuselage. It would have meant a dangerous uphill jump into a roaring wind stream. We decided the best plan was for me to jump into the larger village where the "X" was and then walk over to the radio operator. At least with this plan we could approach the drop site in level flight. From the air, we could plainly see a trail, a narrow brown ribbon, connecting the two villages. The decision made, I went back and stood at the door once again. Before I left, the co-pilot, Lt. Dodo Babb of Dallas, Texas, said, "Good luck, Bill, but remember: The third time is the charm."

"Wonderful friends I have. You guys are always making me feel good."

On this jump I was more nervous than ever before. In the first place, my parachute was just one of the ones lying on the floor of the plane for emergency use. If I survived this jump, in the future I was going to watch my chutes get packed personally. It at least would give me a greater sense of security. I guess I was wondering, too, about how the odds changed every time I took the leap. I stood at the door and watched the green hills unfold under me. And then, for a moment, I stopped worrying about the jump. There soaring beside us was a giant and magnificent eagle.

And before I could get scared again, I got the wake-up call—the bell rang and I stepped out the door.

I must have leaned over and looked down before I pulled the ripcord because I started to somersault through the air. When the chute opened, the canopy came streaming up between my legs and right in front of my nose. When it opened, I was still upside down with my feet all tangled up in the shroud lines. I struggled and twisted, trying to free my feet. If I hit the ground like this, I'd surely break my neck.

Somehow I got my boots free of the lines and righted myself just in time, probably no more than five hundred feet from the ground. I had no time to try and guide the chute. Directly under me was a tall tree with its limbs spread to catch me. Into it I crashed, bouncing from limb to limb until my chute finally caught on a branch, halting my fall. I hung there bruised and dazed, jerking up and down like a toy monkey on a string, my feet only five feet from the jungle floor. I was half-conscious, really not caring if I ever moved again. Where the village was I didn't know, nor did I care at the time.

How long I hung there drowsing between unconsciousness and semi-consciousness, I don't know, but something was pulling on my foot, making me bounce up and down again. It made my head hurt. Then I heard the shouting. I opened my eyes and there stood Joe. Or I should say he was a young Naga boy whom I later named Joe; at the moment he was mainly a surprise.

He had run down from the village and had cut his way to me. Now he was trying to wake me up. He made quite a picture. I guessed him to be between twelve and fourteen, and he wore a mixture of Chinese, British, and American uniforms. He seemed a cheerful kid and happy to find me alive. He helped me down out of my harness, and, while I lay on the spinning ground, waiting, he climbed up the tree and retrieved my chute. Tucking it under his arm, he led me slowly up the hill to his village.

By this time, Bill Davis was frantically trying to fly the big plane right on top of the jungle. Half an hour had passed since I'd jumped, and Bill probably thought I was dead or dying, until he saw the white parachute blossom out on the village mud. On his next pass I waved at him, and he started dropping my equipment.

I sat where Joe had left me, propped against a pole, too weak and miserable to care what happened to the packs that were falling. Joe did, though, and ran like the wind from one pack to the next. At each pack he posted one of his small friends as a guard. But there were more packs than Joe had friends, and, aside from Joe, this village didn't seem too friendly. As fast as the packs hit the ground, the elder men and women of the village ran to them and ripped off the cotton dropping-chutes. Normally I gave them these chutes anyway, as they were of no value once used, and the natives made clothes out of them. But when I saw a couple of natives carry an entire pack into their hut, it was a little too much. I marked the hut in my mind and decided I'd find the chief as soon as I was able and make him get it back for me. I really didn't have too much faith in such action, though. If the chief allowed things like this to happen in his village, he didn't have much control over the inhabitants.

I owed a lot to Joe and his friends, however, since without their help I don't think any of the packs would have been recovered. Little Joe and the other little Joes lugged and dragged the packs over to me. They put the packs in a circle around me, and my little friends formed one around them. In the rear stood the older tribesmen jabbering to each other. They realized quickly that assembled here was more wealth than they could accumulate in a lifetime of hard work. The only thing between them and that goal was me . . . and Joe and his squad of boys.

It was a precarious position. To set them straight, I took out my .45. This was deep backcountry where killings were taken as a matter of course, but I had no intention of killing one of them. Instead I decided on a demonstration: A crow sat perched not ten feet away on a rooftop. I aimed and fired. The tremendous blast of that weapon and the incredibly lucky fact that I hit the bird, blowing it into little pieces, had the desired effect. The natives retired to their homes, to talk things over I imagined.

The pack with the radio in it was opened, and once again I talked to Bill Davis in the plane. "Just once, old man, just once I wish one of you jokers would drop me on the ground. I've been in trees so much lately I feel like a bird." There was great competition among the pilots in the accuracy of their dropping—so I ribbed him a little. He deserved it, I thought.

"If you ever hit the ground, Diebold," Bill squawked

back, "you'd break every bone in your body. I'm simply looking out for your well-being by cushioning your fall."

"Things don't look too hot down here, Bill. The natives have stolen some of our packs and all of the dropping chutes, which is unusual. Which of the packs they took I don't know, but I will tomorrow, and you can drop replacements. O.K.?"

"O.K., Willy. Anything else?"

"Yeah, old man. A Tommy gun would come in handy, I think."

"That bad, huh? Well, you're in," he said. "But it will be dark before I can get back, so tomorrow will have to do. See you then."

My boy Joe was sitting there with a big grin on his face. He definitely liked the army, anybody could see that. He was eyeing my equipment with open admiration. Then he said, "American go bang, bang; Naga go like hell."

At this he and all his little friends laughed uproariously. I guessed their average age, like Joe's, to be between thirteen and fifteen. My friend Joe, speaking English of a sort, was going to be a tremendous help.

I pointed in the direction of the other village, the one I needed to walk to, and asked him, "American there?"

He nodded.

I took out a pencil and notebook and wrote a note to the radio operator. "Will arrive at your village tomorrow to help you in any way possible." I folded the paper and handed it to Joe. I told him to give it to one of his friends and have him run it over to the other American. He did, and the other little boy took off on a dead run. At the rate he started, he'd be faster than Western Union.

Joe's family had a house, and, since his parents seemed as friendly as he was, we moved into that, packs and all. Joe was watching over me like a mother bird over its young. His gang was around all the time. I was truly thankful to the little guy. I don't know what I would have done without him.

That night he put up my jungle hammock, opened the American rations, and cooked dinner for me, himself, his parents, and his friends. Their help was worth all kinds of rations at this point. After dinner, I asked Joe to take me to the chief of the village.

Joe shook his head. "Him no good Naga. Him alla time smoke kahni."

I took the word kahni to mean opium, but I was determined to see him. I wanted to find out what the score was in this village. If it was definitely unfriendly, I wanted to get out and fast. Joe and his little gang would be no match for the whole village. I thought, or hoped, I might be able to persuade—or frighten—the old man into helping me. At least that was the plan.

Joe led me through the mud to another hut, and we went in. Around the fire in the back of the room the usual circle of oldsters lay about, drinking tea and smoking. The guttural gurgle of the pipes and the harsh noise of tea being sipped were as usual—except there wasn't a friendly countenance in the place. Joe pointed out the head man, a grizzled old bird with a couple of long grey hairs stringing down his face. His teeth were all but gone, and the one or two that remained were black and decayed. This hut, too, had an abundance of heads on the wall. It wasn't a very pleasant sight to look at, particularly at a time like this.

The weight of my .45 on my hip gave me a somewhat shaky but small sense of confidence. I approached the fire and stood there, hands on hips, and looked down at the old guy. Joe jabbered something in Naga. The chief took a noisy sip of tea and, gesturing with his pipe, answered Joe angrily.

Joe turned to me, "Him say him no know what him men do."

"The hell he doesn't," I said more to him than to Joe. My voice must have risen when I said it because a couple of the chief's men got up and, fingering their long knives, stood in the background and watched. The skin began to crawl on the back of my neck. But it didn't seem to bother the chief much. He merely lay back and sucked noisily on his pipe, his eyes glazed and complacent.

"Him no damn good," said Joe, and he was right. There wasn't any point in arguing with this hop-headed old fogey, I thought, but I directed Joe: "Tell him that if he harms one hair on my head"—and I gulped when I said it—"I'll have the plane bomb out his village, and soldiers will kill all of his people. If he helps me, I will give him rice and cloth and salt."

Joe and the chief talked for a few minutes, and then Joe turned his eyes on me with a funny look. "Him say him be good Naga if you giv'um kahni."

"To hell with him," I answered. "Tell him again what we'll do if he hurts us."

11

The next morning Joe put one of his friends on guard over our stuff, and with a small pack he and I started out for the other village. Joe said the village was three hours away, and, as usual, it was all uphill.

We walked about an hour and a half when Joe grabbed me by the arm and pulled me into the jungle. I hadn't heard anything, but it wasn't a minute before I, too, heard voices. Down the trail came some natives, and walking in the center of the group was a white man. Joe and I waited until they were beside us, and then I said, "What in the hell are you doing out here?" The guy almost jumped out of his skin.

His name was Johnny Beug, I learned, from "West by God Virginia," as he put it. He was happy to see me, but wondered how I had arrived on the spot so soon. He hadn't seen me parachute into the other village.

We retraced our steps back to Joe's village where we made some coffee, and Johnny and I sat down to talk.

His plane, on which he had been sergeant radio operator, had severe engine trouble, and the crew was ordered
to bail out. Johnny hadn't seen the remainder of the crew
jump, but when he was floating earthward he saw their
parachutes above him. He counted the chutes: pilot, co-
pilot, and engineer, three; they had all made it out. But
the mountain wind currents had blown them all over the
place, and they'd landed far away from one another.

"It was my last flight," Johnny said. "I was sweatin' out
my States-side orders."

"Well, you're safe enough now—I think. It'll just take
you a little longer to get home."

At that point, a native entered the hut. Johnny introduced us. "This is the chief of the village I was in, back up
the trail; he's a good guy and took good care of me."

I stood and bowed, raising both hands to my forehead in
the Naga-style greeting. The chief, chuckling, did the same.
I called Joe over as interpreter. "Tell him the American Army
thanks him for taking care of one of its men. Ask him what
the American Army can give him as thanks."

The chief, Shum Lum, nodded his head in evident
pleasure as he spoke to Joe in Naga. Joe turned to me.
"Him say him want rice, sugar, salt, cloth, and maybe"—
Joe made a circle around his neck with his finger—"for
woman."

Jewelry, apparently. I told Joe to tell him that all he
asked for would be dropped into his village as soon as
Johnny and I hit civilization. In the meantime, though, I
was prepared to pay a rupee a day to him and his men if
they would help us out of the country. The chief nodded

again, and the agreement was sealed. Then Shum Lum joined us for some coffee.

But Johnny had one more piece of valuable information. He handed me a note that read, "I'm Pete the engineer. I'm damned tired and hungry. Come and get me please. Bring food, I'm starved. Pete."

The note had been given to Johnny a couple of days before by one of Shum Lum's men. "Joe," I said, "ask the chief which one of his men brought in this note."

Shum Lum and Joe jabbered a minute, and Joe answered: "Him no this place, him other place—what wanna know?"

"I want to know where his man got this note and anything else the chief may know."

After some more jabbering, Joe turned to me and drew a long breath. This, I knew, would be an effort, taxing his limited ability to speak English, but he did his best. "Him say him man see American 'ummm jungle. American no good." Joe made signs like many cuts on his body. "Him got"—Joe imitated a big knee and limped. "Him say him man make hut. American sleep. Him say American"—Joe imitated writing—"man bring Shum Lum. One sleep, Shum Lum go American, American"—he raised his hands in the air in a gesture of dismissal.

I lay down, closed my eyes, and imitated a man dead, then asked Joe, "American dead, Joe?"

"No, no, him, him . . . ," he stuttered, then began to pretend to be looking for something in a futile attempt to find it. Talking with Joe took a great deal of imagination, but I figured he meant that Shum Lum's man went back to the spot where he had left the engineer sleeping, but the engineer was gone, and that was that. They shouldn't have left him. They didn't realize that an American, one minute operating an intricate piece of mechanism such as an airplane, was no match for the primitive conditions in the jungle the next minute.

"Joe," I told him, "tell the chief I want all the men, women, and children he can get to go look for the American. I will pay all who will work a rupee a day. I will make his village the richest village out here. I will also give a hundred rupees to the man, woman, or child who finds him." I don't know if Joe grasped the idea of a hundred rupees, but I had held up one rupee and then gestured like I was giving out a handful of them, so I think he got the idea. Great excitement followed Joe's translation. The chief nodded again and again, all smiles—he was ready to start.

I held up my hand to quiet all. "Joe, tell Shum Lum I want to go with the best tracker and the best hunter he has in his village to the place where his man saw the American."

The word "tracker" had little Joe stopped for a minute, but when I made a few footprints in the mud and then pretended to follow them, he got the idea. His English may have been a little short of perfect, but he had a quick and ready mind. He suggested we should start right away. "Go soon," he said, but first he made it clear we needed to eat—"Food first, then go." Besides being smart, he had his priorities.

During lunch, which Joe cooked for Shum Lum, his gang, Johnny, and me, the chief explained through Joe that we would go to his village for the men. This village we were in, he told me, was no damn good—as if I didn't know! I could also smell a touch of craftiness. Keeping all the money in the chief's village was good business, especially for the chief.

We decided that Johnny, together with the radio, my .45, and a couple of Joe's chums, would stay with our supplies and contact the search plane when it came over. I wanted Major Hedrick to know what was going on out here. After lunch, we started up the trail in the hot noonday sun.

At four that afternoon, we arrived at Shum Lum's village where we'd spend the night. In an effort to keep up with the fast native pace and not slow down the party, I had packed a light load for myself. As a result I had very little food and no jungle hammock. I had brought mostly medical supplies—hoping for the best. Nevertheless, we had a good dinner; I watched them cook the monkey myself. There was also rice. By this time I was becoming accustomed to the natives' diet, and it didn't faze me much. The Waldorf Astoria was far, far away.

That night, Shum Lum held a religious service or ceremony. It was the first one I had ever seen these people have. It was unusual, and, if I hadn't trusted the chief and Joe so much, I would have been scared to death.

First of all, they tied vegetable matter to all the heads that decorated Shum Lum's house. Then they killed a chicken and sprayed the blood on each of the decorated heads and sprayed a little blood on each other and on me. That bothered me a bit, but it was Shum Lum's house and his ceremony, so I made no objection. Then they squatted before the fire and chanted for hours, it seemed to me. After that, we all moved outside. On the ground, they formed a circle. In the center of the circle they stuck a four-pronged stick, and, in the center of those four prongs, they put an egg, and the chief threw rice in the four directions of the compass. At this the chanting grew in volume and then suddenly ceased. Joe explained: "Shum Lum fixum up good—find American." I nodded, my face long and serious, for it had been a solemn occasion. It had also been, I was surprised to learn, in support of our search. I hoped it would work.

Inside the hut, Joe and I talked. Or rather we talked and gestured our way through what passed for a conversation. He tried to explain a little about their ceremony. The gist of it, or of what I was able to understand, was this: They believed in little spirits that ran all over the place. Some of them were helpful, and some weren't. I had noticed that before taking a drink or eating anything, the natives up here would spill a little of it first. I asked Joe about this and he explained. It seemed there was a pumpkin or a gourd (I'm guessing a little here) lying on the trail. A Naga found it and heard little voices emanating from within. He took out his knife and started to cut it open, but a voice cried out, "Don't cut there; we are crowded in here, and you will kill me." The pumpkin, it seemed, was filled with little spirits.

The native then started to cut it open at another spot, but a little voice called out in terror, "Don't cut there, either, for you will kill me." Then another little voice called out, "Cut it here! You may kill me, but the others will be free to go fight the evil spirits." The native did, and the little spirit was killed, but the remainder were freed. In tribute to that little guy, they always gave him a part of everything they had.

It may have sounded absurd to me, but Joe was dead serious about it, and if he believed it that was good enough for me. You also have to understand that I've filled in a lot where Joe's English and sign language (and a couple scratched drawings on the ground) failed him, but as far as I could get it that's what he told me.

No one in this village was allowed to smoke kahni or opium. Evidently this was a very high-class Naga chief, this Shum Lum. As a result, these natives were more interested in everything, including me.

"Shum Lum, him say where you come?" Joe asked.

"America."

"Shum Lum, him say where America?"

That was a trifle difficult to explain. I tried some water with a piece of bamboo floating on it and blew the bamboo along the surface. Joe looked offended at my ignorance of his vocabulary. "Him boat," he said. "No—" he blew noisily through his lips. "Him go chug, chug."

"O.K., O.K.," I said, "boat go chug, chug to America, fifty sleeps." I held up ten fingers five times. They all looked their astonishment as Joe translated. On a shelf on the wall I saw a jungle apple. I took it and held it up, pointing to one side and said, "Naga sleep here," then turning the apple, I pointed to the other side, "America here." I don't know if they quite understood what it all meant, but they seemed satisfied, and for an hour or two afterward they talked of "American" and "America." Now and then one of them would pick up the apple, examining it as if to find America there.

The next morning we started off to where one of the men had last seen the engineer. The whole village started out, as a matter of fact. There must have been fifty men, women, and children fanning out over the countryside. How many of them would actually hunt was questionable, but if only half of them would that was still a lot of searchers.

In my party were Joe and Shum Lum, of course. Added to these two faithfuls were two of the best hunters in the village. They wore nothing but loincloths and carried old muzzle loading guns. I hadn't seen anything like those guns since I had been to the Smithsonian. One of them was actually a flint-lock model. Where we started, the village was halfway up the side of a mountain. It was really a high baby, and the air was becoming thin, and I found breathing a problem. We paused once at twelve o'clock while the natives ate some cold rice they had brought along and I ate a D ration bar. It was a short pause, too short. Long ago, my canteen had been drained dry, and so far we hadn't run into any mountain streams where I could refill it. Eating highly concentrated chocolate when your throat is dry and you're famished for water, I found, isn't one of the pleasures of life.

It was two o'clock in the afternoon when we reached the lean-to the native had built for the engineer. The jungle was thick here, and obviously the American had no knife for we could easily see where he'd pushed his way through the heavy brush. Why the natives had left him on his own that day is a little hard to explain. I think it was something like I said before: The jungle is their home, and they see no danger in it. If a man wants to wander off by himself, that's his business, and he may go where he likes just so long as he commits no crime. When the engineer was gone, Shum Lum, I guess, figured he knew what he wanted, and it was no further concern.

The going became very slow now as we picked our way along, following his tracks. I can say that, although I wanted to find that boy as soon as possible, I was happy at the delay. After all, when a parachutist hits the ground, he's going about fifteen feet per second. It was like jumping off of a twelve-foot wall into the top of that tree and bouncing through by ricocheting off limbs. My muscles and bones were more than slightly sore.

The engineer, we could tell by his trail, was having a tough go of it. Hell, we were having a tough time just trying to go where he'd already gone. One good thing, he did have a system. He wasn't just wandering aimlessly around in the woods; he was following the ridge line above a roaring mountain stream. He'd discovered water and was staying with it, which was wise. I for one was most happy, as was my parched throat.

When we first came to the water, we were above it. I knew how that engineer felt when he saw it down there. We slid crazily down the same place he had to get at it. It was a crystal clear, ice-cold stream. We all sank our faces into it and drank deeply. A gang of mules would have made less noise at the job.

Here we ran into difficulty, though, losing the lad's trail for a while. Then one of the natives discovered that he had retraced his steps to the top of the ridge again. The stream was a roaring mad thing, impossible to walk in. The thick jungle hugged the edges, making it out of the question to fight our way through there. The top of the ridge above the stream was his only alternative. Following him again, we came to a spot where he had spent a night. He had gathered some dried leaves and put them in the hollow of a tree. Doubled up, he tried to sleep in there. A little later, the hunter in charge stopped and pointed out to me where he'd eaten grass. Then he found another of the engineer's sleeping spots. On and on we went over the roughest type of terrain. We were covering in one day more than he had been able to cover in five, but then we had knives, and there were more of us who could trade shifts on the cutting end. Still, progress was a rapid snail's pace.

Four o'clock passed, and still we didn't stop for the night. Then five and six and seven went by, and still Shum Lum kept going. I was so tired I was dragging along behind, half in a daze much of the time. Usually on the trail all treks are finished by four in the afternoon so a camp can be made before darkness. At seven thirty we were still following a barely perceptible trail, and it was dark. I had left my flashlight with Johnny back in the village. The only thing I had that would give light was my cigarette lighter. I handed this to Shum Lum and showed him how to work it. He held it down near the ground, and he could see the footprints of the engineer. With that tiny glow, we continued. It was an incongruous sight to see: the ancient and the modern, a loinclothed native bending over a modern cigarette lighter on the trail.

Finally the lighter ran out of fluid, and we had to stop. All of us were exhausted, and we dropped in our tracks. We built a feeble fire for a little warmth and protection, but it went out in a few minutes, unnoticed, for we were all already asleep on the ground.

At the first streak of dawn, we set off again. By all figuring, we shouldn't be too far behind him. I hoped we would reach him in time. He was probably in a bad way. The top of the ridge had become so thick with jungle he'd been unable to push his way through, terrifically handicapped without a knife. At the bottom of the ridge the stream grumbled, still swift and dangerous. It had been his only alternative and a dangerous one. From the top of the ridge to the stream below was a straight drop of some two hundred feet. Near the top edge, the roots of trees extended beyond the wall of the ridge.

How our native knew, I'll never be able to tell, but it was over the edge of the cliff and down on these roots the engineer had climbed. It seemed impossible that he could make it in his obviously weakened condition. I looked below fully expecting to see his body smashed on a rock, but it wasn't. He had climbed along that sheer cliff from root to root. We followed his scrape marks on each root. I didn't dare look down, for it was a terrifying sight. Slowly we edged along for about a half a mile to where the jungle became less dense above. Here he had climbed back up to the top of the ridge again.

His trail began to look fresher, and following him grew easier. The ridge became lower, bending down to the stream below. Here our engineer had found a much-used trail. I couldn't believe it, but even I could see it was the same trail that led from Shum Lum's village to the one where Johnny was.

We had made a very large circle.

We followed along this trail, finally coming to him as he stumbled along on his slow, weary way. He was in pretty horrible condition. His hair was matted and tangled with burrs, his clothing all but torn off. His shoes had fallen apart. His face was gaunt, as he stared at us with unbelieving eyes. He sat down where he was and said, "Thank God!" I gave him a quick examination and found his body a mass of old and new cuts. Pus-filled leech bites were very much in evidence.

The natives quickly built a litter, and we took him on to the village. He'd almost made it himself, but we'd been good insurance and damned welcome. At Shum Lum's house, we made him a bed, and Joe put water on to boil. The engineer lay there with his eyes closed while I cut off his clothing—or what was left of it. After washing them clean, I dusted all the open cuts with sulfa powder. Using a razor blade sterilized with iodine, I opened quite a few that were covered with scabs filled with pus. Then I lightly rubbed his sore body with olive oil. Untangling his hair was impossible, so I gave him a crew cut as well as a shave. This done, he drank a light broth. After that, he lay back, smoking a cigarette, and started talking.

"Exactly where am I?"

"Well, you're not quite in the heart of civilization," I grinned, "but you're near it. In a few days when you feel better, we'll take a slow trip out of here."

"How'd you get here?"

"I jumped in."

"Well, I'll be damned. Something new has been added in the way of jungle rescue. Have you been able to find the rest of our crew?"

"There are two still missing, the pilot and co-pilot. Your friend Johnny Beug is in the next village, and I'm certain we'll be able to find the other two," I told him, wishing it were true but doubting it.

"By the way, what's your name? All we know you by is the note signed 'Pete the engineer.'"

"That's me, all right. I'm Corporal Peter Ercig, the plane's engineer—or was. I'm not too sure it's the same Pete anymore."

"What part of the States are you from, Pete?"

"Oh, it's a little town near Albany, New York. You wouldn't remember the name if I told you."

"Well, I'll be darned. My wife lives in Albany. It's a pretty good town."

This was all Pete needed. We talked of Albany and the States until he finally fell asleep. I didn't think it a good idea to ask him anything in connection with his days in the jungle yet, for he was still suffering from shock and exposure. There would be plenty of time for that when he felt better. Sleep and food were wonderful restoratives. I wanted Pete to get plenty of both in the coming days. I felt almost as exhausted as he looked.

Joe and I went down to the village stream and took baths. While I had a shave, little Joe whipped back to the hut and cooked a delicious chicken dinner. That was the first meal we had eaten in two days, and it really hit the spot.

After dinner we sat around the fire again. But things were different. The natives were in a state of high elation. From my bag I had given every man, woman, and child in the village a big silver rupee. To the chief I gave a hundred, and to every member of our tracking party I gave five. About fifty or sixty dollars for saving Pete's life. We would have spent a million, if necessary, and even then it would have been worth the cost.

Not even weariness could stop the natives from having a little celebration that night—and of course I had to join them. In the corner a flute player blew his eerie music, and much rice, wine, and beer was in evidence. These people had a funny sense of humor. They would chase each other about the floor on their hands and knees, imitating dogs barking, pigs grunting, and chickens cackling. Most of us sat on the side and laughed until the tears rolled down our faces. It was really a funny sight to see grown men galloping around the floor after one another, grunting like pigs.

One of the young bucks was pretending he was a cow. I ran over and pretended to milk him, using a can of condensed milk to create realism. The natives went into hysterics. It was all great fun. Later, when the party quieted down a bit, the chief made a little speech. Joe interpreted.

"Him say you O.K. American. Him want make you Naga chief—give sticker." The chief handed me a long spear, the entire thing decorated with bunches of hair that had been dyed red. The back of my neck crawled. This looked to be human hair, scalp and all.

I thanked the chief as well as I could, through Joe. Then he handed me a pair of tiny earrings. They were made of a piece of thin wire with two clay beads hanging from the bottom of them.

Joe answered my incredulous look: "All O.K. Naga have 'um." Joe pointed to his own earrings.

Me with earrings on? I'd never live it down. But the chief was honoring me; if I refused, I might not even live. The decision wasn't hard to make.

The chief put small holes in the lobes of my ears and inserted the earrings. They were small holes, but when he was putting them in it felt like he was digging the Holland Tunnel. In lieu of a needle, he used a sharp sliver of bamboo. It hurt like hell, but anything to keep the natives happy was my motto.

Through all this Pete had been sleeping. Now he woke up, probably from my yelling, and said he was hungry again. This time, unlike when I had been taking care of Greenie Collins, I had Joe working for me. Poor Joe—it was his job to get up every hour in the night and make Pete some soup. I would have been happy to do it, but I spent the night sleeping.

The next morning, I sent Joe back to the other village with a note to Johnny Beug: "We have found Corporal Ercig. Please notify Search and Rescue of that fact. He is in poor shape, but not dangerously so. Tell search plane to drop shoes, size 10½ D, and large set of khaki clothing as well as socks and underwear. Also tell them I need olive oil and sulfa powder. Have them drop a hundred pounds of rice and two hundred rupees. I want all these drops made into this village. Tell them we are continuing the search for pilot and co-pilot. Pete and I will join you in your village as soon as Pete is able to make the trip."

Late that evening, Joe returned with a note from Johnny. "Search plane reports the pilot has been brought into American airstrip by natives and is O.K. No word of co-pilot. Your drops will be made tomorrow morning. Hurry back. I'm safe enough with all this armament they have dropped, but I'm itching to get goin'."

The next day the plane came over and the drops came. I didn't have my radio, so I had Joe cut up pieces of bamboo about three feet long and split in half. The inside of bamboo is virgin white, and with these white strips I paneled out: DIEBOLD—DROP HERE.

After the plane dropped the packs, it circled around again and dropped a streamer. The note was from the pilot, Willy Watt of Thomasville, Georgia. "Better come out, old man of the mountains. Jinx Falkenburg is going to put on a U.S.O. show at the base." I read his note, and for the joke of it I paneled back: HAVE OWN JINX HERE SLIGHTLY TANNED.

I never lived that one down. Willy, it seems, went to a dance that night at the Officers Club and told all the guys what a good time I was having in the jungle. No amount of argument after that could convince those fellows that the Naga Hills weren't full of dusky beauties. It had been a lot of trouble paneling that message, but from that time on I always had a sufficiency of volunteers to jump when the alert was in Naga country.

12

Days flew by in such rapid succession that I soon lost track of them. Daily changes of the dressings on Pete's sores and applications of sulfa worked wonders. I was rather proud of my medical treatments being so successful. Every day the sun was out I moved him onto the chief's porch, covered him with olive oil, and made him take a sun bath. His condition rapidly improved, and Joe and I began making plans for his evacuation. As he grew stronger, we made him walk a bit, a little farther each day. Not only did it improve his stamina, but it broke in his new G.I. shoes as well.

During these days of convalescence, he told me the story of what had happened to him. He'd spent a total of ten days alone, wandering around in the jungle. It wasn't the longest time on record—Collins had spent twenty-two days in the bush—but it was too long to go without food or a dry place to sleep during the monsoon rains. He had no knife to cut his way through the brush. After he landed in his parachute, he'd taken out his jungle kit and started making his way down the mountain. When he reached the bottom, he found a very noisy, swift stream with the water boiling over slippery rocks. He had tried to follow the edge of the stream, but the jungle clung so close to its edge he found this impossible. It looked to him like the other side of the stream would be the better proposition, so he had crossed. Unluckily, his feet slipped on the rocks and in he went. His jungle equipment was swept downstream, and lost. He stood in the middle of the stream, no knife, no food, nothing but nerve . . . and he had plenty of that.

A couple of days later, he ran into some natives. He wasn't certain whether he and the crew had bailed out over enemy territory, but since the natives seemed friendly he decided to write a note and wait to see what developed. They built him a lean-to where he stayed for two days, then he moved on. He thought they wouldn't come back, and, also, he'd noticed Oriental writing on one of the native's guns. He didn't know whether it was Japanese or Chinese, but it made him uneasy.

He pushed his way for six more days and then saw us. He'd been alone so long, he said, that he began to hear train whistles in the distance and voices calling him, and he thought we were part of that setup. I knew exactly what he meant, for it had happened to me, too, on more than one occasion, when I was too tired to move a muscle but had to keep going. The jungle is a mysterious place and makes many noises, noises multiplied by a lonely and delirious mind.

The day arrived when both Pete and I thought he was ready to travel. It was a three hour hike over to the other village—we'd been sending Joe and his friends back and forth nearly every day to check on Johnny for us—but it took us six hours. From this I figured it would take us a long, long time to hike out of this country. Well, I had nothing else to do: As soon as I got out I went right back in again, so we might as well take our time. From Pete's point of view, the slower we went the easier it was for him. Only Johnny would suffer from the delay, but that couldn't be helped.

Johnny had heard from the natives that we were coming and was on hand to greet us, a welcoming committee of one and armed to the teeth by the air drops. He and Pete had a lot of things to talk about, and a bull session ensued while Joe knocked out the dinner. Shum Lum and some of his men were with us to act as guides and to carry some of Uncle Samuel's equipment that we'd been dropped. I was sorry to tell Johnny that none of our searching parties had been able to find the co-pilot. Men had been out every day and had covered the local jungle from the air as well as they were able, but no luck. It had been the co-pilot's first trip over the Hump, Johnny told me. It was a rough deal, but we'd done everything within our power to find him.

"He might turn up at one of the airbases with a native," I told them. "Some of you guys who've been jumping out of expensive airplanes have a habit of doing that." We all hoped so.

The next day we started out again, our party augmented now by Johnny and a couple of Joe's buddies. I didn't mind the extra cost of having them along; they had been so much help. They made sort of a juvenile gang, and I was happy to have them on my side. For protection alone, they were well worth it. And because they were full of fun, they were entertaining as well.

Through this country, Merrill's Marauders had hiked on their way to defeat the Japanese. Prior to that, the Chinese and British had been fighting the Japs over this same ground. Shum Lum had been with them. He and many of the people from the surrounding country had been hired by both the British and the Chinese to cut trail and to act as guides and scouts. This is how little Joe had learned to speak English, by being a camp mascot.

Every once in a while either Joe or Shum Lum would stop and point to a piece of terrain ahead and say, "Here two British finish—twenty Japs finish," ten fingers twice. Then again at another spot, "Here"—ten fingers— "Chinese finish"—pause with meaningful look, then ten fingers four times—"Japs finish." Some nights we slept in old abandoned Chinese camps and some nights in British camps. Old foxholes and machine gun revetments, all overgrown now but still wicked to look at, were scattered in the jungle.

It seemed strange to think that battles were fought way out here, so far from practically everything. The country was so quiet and peaceful, and the mountains so lovely. Where we stood, so far from their homes in these fields, men had died who would never be heard of, not to mention commemorated. This gorgeous piece of country—and when I wasn't sweating or fighting leeches, I had to admit it had its good points—took on a new feeling after seeing these signs of war. The war part of it, though, somehow seemed grisly and foreboding, pockmarked as the countryside was with shell holes and old gun emplacements, rapidly being reclaimed by the undergrowth. I wondered how long the jungle would remember the men who had fallen here.

The trails, on the other hand, were wonderful. The British had cut them wide and neat. At one time they had zigzagged up the steep mountain slopes. It was the long, but more sensible way to do it, though not as far as the Nagas were concerned. For them, the shortest way over a mountain is from the bottom straight over the top, and that's the way they climbed, trail or no trail. All the curves in the old British trail were grown over. The Nagas completely ignored them and had been, for a year, climbing straight up the mountains disdainfully crossing the British trail when, and only when, it swung back into their direct path. It was very exasperating for Johnny, Pete, and me to see how much easier our climb would have been had they followed the better engineered road.

In spite of the sometimes difficult terrain, it was a lazy man's journey. When we came to a good-size river, we'd stop for a day and swim and fish. It was rather marvelous fishing way back there in that virgin country. If only we'd brought along a trout pole and flies, everything would have been perfect. As it was, we sat lazily on rocks in the sun and caught with a bent pin and some string enough one-pound fish to feed us all. They were some kind of sucker fish and darn good to eat. The natives dug up roots that tasted like potatoes. Although we made no contact with the rescue plane on the trip out, we ate well and had a great vacation.

One night when we were camped on the sand beside a river, I could have sworn I felt, or somehow knew, something was near me. Later I heard a tremendous crashing of bamboo and the scream of a monkey. Suddenly, again, all was quiet, too quiet. In the morning, we looked under our jungle hammocks in amazement. Huge tiger prints made their way up to each of our hammocks, stopped, and then turned away.

The prints of those paws were at least eight inches in diameter.

13

Major Hedrick sat at his desk puffing on that perpetual cigar stub. It was evening, and the briefing of the pilots for the next day's missions had just been completed, and I'd been asked to stay behind—again. I was a regular now. While I'd been gone on my last trip, the major had had me permanently assigned to the outfit. I was now officially a member of the 1352nd Army Air Forces Base Unit (Search and Rescue). I was happy about the assignment and glad to know they were going to let me stick around a little longer.

For a moment we just sat there, listening to the pilots' voices as they made their way back to their bashas. By now I had gotten to know the major well enough to wait until he was ready to share whatever was on his mind. He looked at me through the screen of his cigar smoke, and, speaking half to me and half to himself, he mused, "Ya know, it must be a little rough out there sometimes for somebody all by himself. Hum-n. If this sort of thing is going to become a regular practice, Diebold, I think you should have an assistant."

We sat in silence. I had no suggestions to offer. So far everything had gone well enough. But I could see he had a point: A little company wouldn't be too bad on some of those lonely nights when there was no one to talk to except the opium-smoking natives. From the standpoint of personal protection, nothing had ever happened to make me feel any more help was needed, but then I wasn't running this show, and what the major said was the law.

When he saw I wasn't going to say anything, he took it up again: "Yep, I think that's a good idea, and I believe I have just the man." He reached for the phone.

"Hello, charge to quarters? This is Major Hedrick. I want Sergeant Brenner to report to my office immediately. Yes, that's right, now."

He hung up the phone and turned to me. "He's a new man who's just reported to the unit. He's been in combat a couple of times and seems as tough as they come. Look him over, and see what you think. But you have the final say-so on this, Diebold. If you think he's O.K. and he'll do, then you've got a partner."

Within five minutes Technical Sergeant James Brenner reported. I couldn't believe my eyes. Was the major off his nut, or was this some kind of a joke? Sergeant Brenner was gray-haired and had to be over forty. Hell, with all these young pilots around here I felt pretty ancient myself, and I wasn't even thirty yet. This guy came from another generation.

The major looked the new guy over. "Pull up a chair, sergeant, and let's have a talk. What do you think you're best qualified to do around here?"

Sergeant Brenner's face split into a grin. "Me, I don't go for this non-combatant stuff, sir. It may be necessary and all that, but, me, I want some shootin' an' stuff goin' on. This camp life'ud drive me nuts . . . sir."

As they talked, I observed him, and the closer look was reassuring. He wasn't young, but that he was tough and hard as a rock was easy to see. He was short, but broad and straining bunches of muscle writhed up and down his arm. There wasn't a pound of fat on him, and I guessed his weight to be around two hundred—he was a solid man. His gray hair was close-cropped, and his nose was flat from seven years in the ring, I later found. He looked like a man who could handle himself in a scrap.

He talked with an accent that sounded like a conglomeration of Chicago Loop, Brooklynese, and Pennsylvania Dutch. It was something entirely new in accents, and sometimes what he said was hard to understand. I didn't know it then, but later he was to have me talking in much the same way—it was as contagious as a southern accent.

"Well, what do you think, Diebold?" the major asked.

Hell! I didn't know. The sergeant looked like a good man, but a personality clash out in the jungle would be a hard thing to overcome. But the major was waiting for me to say something, so I asked the sergeant, "Sarge, if you were given a job that was tough, a job no one else wants, a job as close to combat as it can get and sometimes even gets to be combat, a job that meant a definite risk of that neck of yours at least once a month, and most of the time more often than that, would that satisfy your desire for shootin' and stuff like that?"

He looked at me for a long minute. Now *he* was sizing *me* up, and I probably didn't look too good. I had just arrived back that evening and hadn't shaved; my shorts and T-shirt were ripped and dirty; my legs and arms were covered with bruises and cuts. A couple or three jungle ulcers had started eating their way to the bones of my legs. Here I was trying to figure him out, and I didn't make much of an advertisement for the job myself.

"I've heard about you, lieutenant, and, if you're asking if I'll jump with you and rescue these guys, then I'm the man for the job." He was dead serious and didn't mean to be bragging one bit. Regardless of his age, he thought he was the man, and I was inclined to agree with him.

We shook hands. "O.K., Sarge, we'll take a crack at it together once and see how it goes."

That began what was the damnedest and best friendship between two men that ever existed.

The next day I made a list of the things Sergeant Brenner would need, gave it to him, and that was the last I saw of him for a week. I had begun to think he'd changed his mind and run for it. Then the alert came.

A ship's crew had run into trouble coming back over the Hump, and, there being no other course to take, they'd bailed out. Our search ships crisscrossed the probable area of bailout for days with no luck when into an airstrip in Burma walked two of the crew. Out of nowhere the sarge showed up, we got our briefing, and he and I took off to meet the crewmen. Three of them had been aboard that aircraft, and it was the third man we were looking for now.

Our plane picked up the two men who had walked out, and at their direction we flew over the valley into which they'd parachuted. They'd been lucky and had landed beside each other. They'd seen the third man's chute open but that was the last they did see of him. This, of course, isn't too unusual. He might have landed thirty yards away, and in that jungle they could never have seen him.

After an hour or so of circling and hunting, we spotted their two chutes hanging in trees where they had left them. Off in the distance, not more than a mile, was the third chute, also hanging in a tree. Captain Jack Knight of Nashville, Georgia, the pilot of our Doug, called me forward into the cockpit.

"Well, there she is, Bill. It's pretty rugged stuff with no clearing that I can see. It's sure to be a tree landing if you go. How about walking into it the same way those two men walked out?"

"That's a good idea, Jack, but it would take us a week to make it in there, and maybe the boy needs help now. I think we'll jump to him if it's O.K. with you."

"It's your neck, chum, and you can use it anyway you want."

Captain Howard McCracken of Jacksonville, Illinois, the co-pilot, turned to me. "Are you nuts, man? That's no place for a man to walk around in, let alone jump into. Whaddaya want, the medal of honor or something?"

"Not a bad idea. Put me in for it when I get back, will you?" We both laughed, and I turned to Jack: "Give us about five minutes to get into our chutes. You won't be able to drop any food or stuff in that mess, so I'll take my radio and some food with me when I go."

"Good luck and good huntin', you damn fool," McCracken said as I left the cockpit.

Then I remembered Brenner. What an initiation to parachute jumping this was going to be for him. He was lying in the back of the ship, pale as a ghost.

"Come on, old man, this is where we get off," I said.

"Thanks, bub. All the twistin' and turnin' this plane is doin' has me sick as a dog—lemme out."

We climbed into our chutes, stuffed our pockets and emergency packs with food, strapped on our jungle knives, and stood ready at the door. Again we were using a new and different type of a chute. These had an auxiliary chute on our chest in case of an emergency. It made us—me, at least—feel better. There was only one problem: In the air, the main chute was deployed by lifting up the chest chute with the left hand and sliding the right under it and pulling the ripcord. It was complicated, and it was going to be difficult to coordinate all those things while falling through the air.

At the door Brenner crowded me close; we wanted to be as near each other as possible when we hit the ground. The bell rang.

I stepped out into space, counted a hurried one-two-three, lifted up the chest chute, found the ripcord with my right hand, and pulled. Brenner took a little longer, but when our chutes opened we were right beside each other.

"How do you like it?" I called to him.

"It's the second greatest thrill I've ever had. I hope we don't get blown back to Assam."

He was right. The ground was whizzing by us at a great clip. A steady wind was blowing us far from the hung-up chute we were trying to land on. How we would ever find it now was the sixty-four dollar question.

But there was little time to worry about that as the ground came up fast. I had a nice, easy landing. In a tree, of course, but my chute caught when my feet were about six inches off the ground, and I didn't hit a limb on the way through. But poor Brenner hadn't fared as well. It was a good thing he was tough and hard. The top limb of a tree had collapsed his chute when he was still about twenty feet above the ground, and down he fell.

"Jeez," he said when he regained focus, "do ya always hit that hard?" We sat there for a minute while the sarge shook the cobwebs out of his brain.

"We're in a helluva mess," I grumbled. "We not only don't know where the chute is, we don't know where we are."

I pulled out the little aerial on the radio and called Jack Knight in the ship above us. He came on the air: "Well, we didn't miss it much, not more than two or three miles. That wind must have been really something," he said.

"It was, but we're both in one piece anyway. Now which way is the chute from where we landed?"

He gave me a compass heading and told me he would have a liaison plane come over in the morning to guide us.

We started cutting our way through the jungle. Here it wasn't too tough, and we made good time. At four o'clock we came to a slow-running stream. It was awfully muddy, but the first sign of water we'd seen. It looked like a good place to spend the night. We hacked out a spot about twenty by twenty feet along the stream's edge. In the center of this clearing we stuck up a long bamboo pole. Over this we draped a parachute and staked down the shroud lines. It looked, when completed, much like an American Indian teepee.

Out in the stream we put some bamboo fish traps, modeling them after the ones I had seen the natives make. They worked, too; in an hour we had a dozen small fish, enough for an evening meal.

That night it rained, and rained hard. The teepee was some protection, but it kept us far from warm and dry. All it seemed to do was to granulate the big rain drops into little ones. We later learned that if two parachutes are draped over the center pole in the same manner the tent is completely waterproof.

The sarge and I rolled up into a parachute for the night. We had a small fire going inside our teepee, and it blazed merrily. The rain beat a steady tattoo on the cloth overhead. It wasn't exactly the type of home I'd recommend to a weekend camper, but it was better than lying in the rain. We lay in silence, watching the fire and thinking. My mind wandered to the fellow we were looking for. What would he be doing on a night like this?

"What would who be doing where?" the sarge asked.

"Oh, I was just wondering how well off the guy we're looking for is tonight."

"If he's anything like us, he's wet as hell."

"Say, Sarge, you never did tell me where you're from in the States."

"Here and there, lieutenant," he said. "Mostly from Chicago, I guess you'd say, but I been in the Army for ten years, and a guy kinda forgets about civilian stuff after that length of time. Before that I was in the ring for a few years—'Shifty' Brenner they called me 'cause I could fight with either a right or a left stickin' in their faces. Pretty soon, though, ya get fed up on that, so I got mixed up in the produce business and a couple of other things, then I joined the Army."

Here's a character, I thought. It was going to be tough sledding for me to keep up with a guy like that.

"What gives with tomorrow?" he asked.

"I think a liaison plane will be over to guide us as we try to cut our way over to the chute."

"Whadda we do if the guy didn't hang around his chute but took off through the jungle?"

"Well, if he used a knife, we can follow the trail he left behind, but if he didn't it will be a lot tougher. I wish Shum Lum were here—he's one of the Naga who helped me on my last trip—'cause we'll have to follow his tracks."

"Now I'm goin' to be an Indian," the sarge said. "Cripes, everything happens to ya in this man's army."

I barely heard him, though. It had been a big day, and sleep was catching me, tugging me off to oblivion.

14

In the morning the liaison plane, a small, single-engine L-5, saw our parachute tent in the clearing and buzzed us, its tiny motor roaring protest at the added effort. The pilot was a basha friend of mine, Lt. Dock Hudson of Greenville, South Carolina.

"You aren't far away, but it sure looks like tough country," he said on the radio. "There are two ways to go: first, the direct way, which is the shortest but will take a lot of cutting; second, follow the stream you are on, and it will junction with another farther down that will lead you almost to the tree the chute is in. The only trouble with that route is it's a hell of a distance. Which way do you want to go?"

"We'll go the shortest way, Dock. What's the compass bearing?"

"I'll fly the course a couple of times and get the heading. Wait a minute."

We watched him fly off in the distance, waggle his wings, turn back, and come over us.

"Did you see where I waggled my wings?" he asked. "Well, that's where the chute is."

"Hell, Lieutenant, that ain't far," Brenner said. "Let's get goin'."

We crossed the stream and started to cut our way through the brush. Here it wasn't hard, only tall elephant grass, easy to get lost in, but also easy to walk through. That piece of luck didn't last long though; in a couple of minutes we ran into bamboo.

I've heard bamboo called rattan and a couple of other names; all I know about it is it grows thick and was real work trying to cut a path through it. We started to cut. First the sarge took a whack at it, and then I would. The old stuff had died and the new growth had pushed its way right on through the dead stuff above. It made a tangled wall of solid bamboo. We'd hack for about two minutes and then move forward a step. The sun was out, and in this stuff there was no breeze, and the jungle was like an oven.

Two hours went by, then three, and still we hacked and beat at that wall. The little plane droned steadily overhead calling down bearings as we veered too much one way or the other—until he left us to go for more gas.

Up in the ship, Dock had watched the brush move and could tell where we were cutting. That little plane had been a great help since we were cutting blind. Still, we couldn't waste the time waiting for him to come back, so on and on we cut. My back ached, and my arms were like lead. The sarge swore lustily as he swung the machete. He wanted to do all the cutting. One would think that for him the whole business of living centered on the battle of the bamboo wall.

In a while we came to an overgrown, dried-up stream bed. Lying flat on our stomachs, we were able to ease along under the growth of jungle above. It seemed like hours went by with our faces buried in the stinking mud, squirming along at a snail's pace. Our little mud track led us to a larger stream where we could stand up straight, the first time in days, it felt. We started to walk down this stream, but the bottom was mud, and we were soon sinking into our knees. The water was a dark, chocolate brown, but we refilled our canteens and dropped a couple of water purification tablets into it. It would be torture walking through water, unable to drink any of it. The halizone in our canteen water would take thirty minutes to purify it to the drinking point.

Walking in water to our waists with mud to our knees was a hard grind. Pulling one foot out of the stuff forced the other down deeper, then pulling that one out forced the other one deeper yet. It was like walking down stairs made of sticky glue. The further we went, the deeper we got mired until we could go no farther. Finally, I stopped my forward struggle and just stood there. I watched the waterline on my shirt. "My God, we're sinking."

"You ain't just a kiddin', lieutenant. Let's get the hell out of this stuff. It's like quicksand."

"Sarge," I told him, "cut out that lieutenant stuff, will ya? Some day you're going to want to tell me something in a hurry, and by the time you get all that out I'll be a dead pigeon."

"Sure, Bill, whatever you say," he said, "but give me a hand, or haven't you noticed I'm up to my chest in this stuff and still goin' down?"

Overhead was a tree limb. If I could reach that, I might be able to pull him and myself clear, but I'd have to work fast, or Brenner would be breathing mud by the time I could help him. I reached up and could barely get my fingers around the branch and pull it down to me. I was hoping it would hold the weight of both the mud and me. It did. I made the bank and shoved the limb back to the sarge. He caught hold of it, and I pulled. Finally, after much struggle, he was out. We sat there covered from head to foot with the smelly, gooey stuff, as miserable a pair as I've ever seen. Then the plane came over again. Luckily we'd been able to hang onto the radio.

"Dock, this isn't the way to get to that chute. The jungle is too thick to cut our way, and this stream we're on isn't a stream at all but quicksand or something. How about another idea, old man?"

"The only other way is to go back to where you were this morning and start over again," he answered. "The other way I told you about is the only other step I can see to take, but it's a long way around."

"All right, Dock, we'll cut our way back, but you had better stick around to guide us. We didn't make much of a trail coming this way."

"Guide you? Hell, I don't even know where you are down there."

"O.K. Come back tomorrow morning; we'll be down the stream we camped on last night. And bring some cigarettes, will you?"

The plane flew off, and Brenner and I started to scramble along the edge of the bank, making our way back.

Somehow we found our old cuttings and made our way to the parachute tent again. This was taking too long, and we needed to get after that boy, wherever he was. We packed the parachutes over our shoulders and made our way downstream. About six o'clock we came to what we thought was the junction of the two streams that Dock had mentioned that morning. There was a small clearing there, so again we built camp and put out fish traps.

We'd just completed putting up the parachute teepee for the night when a Doug flew over. I called to it on the radio. It was a search ship on its way home from a mission. Captain Bill Davis was the pilot, and he heard my call and spotted our campsite.

"What's going on, Bill?" he asked.

"Well, it's this way," I said. "Things don't look too bright. Brenner and I had a tough time trying to get to that chute, and we're hungry as hell. You wouldn't happen to have any food aboard, would you?"

"I do, but whether I can drop it into that little rat-hole you're living in is a horse of a different color, but I'll take a crack at it for you."

The sarge and I watched the Doug circle lazily and make a pass or two over us.

"Bill is getting his bearings for the drop, Jim," I said to Brenner, both of us by now having dropped the rank.

"Here comes our chow. Best watch where it goes because if he misses us it'll be plenty hard to find in this jungle."

The plane shot over us once again and out of the cargo door blossomed a white chute—our dinner being delivered. We watched the chute descend.

"Run like hell, Jim!" I yelled. The drop was almost too perfect. If we had stayed where we were it would have landed in our laps. As it was, it knocked our tent completely down.

Brenner grunted from his perch in the jungle foliage. "Is that guy a pilot or a bombardier, and is he on our side?"

Bill was laughing when he spoke. "Put 'er right on the store for you, didn't I, boy?"

"Some joke. You damn near put it in my pocket. After that one you had better drop us some clean underwear." He was still laughing. "What's so funny?" I asked.

"That's a case of mountain rations, I dropped you. Do you think you can use them? There isn't a mountain in sight as far as I can see."

"Funny, real funny. But thanks for the food anyway. We'll be able to cook it; what do you think mountain rations are—eggs built with a tilt?"

"No," he came back, "I thought it was all lean meat for use on the sides of hills only."

"Corn," I answered, "Strictly corn!"

"See you at dinner time tomorrow," I heard him say as the plane disappeared, "and get to work."

"'Get to work,'" I said to Brenner. "And he calls that work sitting up there pushing buttons in an airplane—phooey!"

That night the unusual happened; it hailed. Yes, in the heart of North Burma, it hailed. It was as unbelievable as snow in July in New York. "My God," Brenner said. "Everything happens to us. All we need now is to have a tornado hit."

"Don't say that," I yelled above the noise of hailstones rattling on the parachute, "or it will damn well happen."

When the hail finally turned to rain again, Brenner and I went out into it and took showers. We both smelled like a couple of Nagas with that mud all over us. After the shower we had a delicious dinner of dehydrated soup, potatoes, and Spam. I, for one, would have preferred the mud-sucking fish, but it was a change.

In the morning we started up the side stream. All went well for half an hour, then the pools began to deepen. Finally I walked into one and disappeared. With the parachute tied to my back, I was too heavy to swim, and I was unable to get the pack off under water. Brenner proved his value by reaching down and grabbing me by the hair and pulling me out. We were now even on this saving business. Already the major's plan to team us up had proved itself.

We could go no farther. The thick jungle crowded the vertical bank, and the water was too deep. We cut some bamboo and tried to build a boat, but the bamboo we were able to get to for cutting was too thin to hold our weight. Then I remembered the rubber boat. So we stood there in the water with leeches dropping on us from the brush overhead and waited for Dock to show up. In a short while he flew over, and I called him.

"Dock, do you think you could go back to the base and get the rubber raft and drop it in here? This thing is too deep to walk through, and the bamboo is too small for us to use in building a raft."

"Sure. Sit tight, and I'll be back in an hour or two."

"O.K., my lad, but hurry! This thing has taken too long already."

True to his word, he was back in an hour, his single-engine L-5 trailed by our Doug. Bill Davis was flying again, and after a couple of trial runs—which included finding us—he dropped the boat right into the stream.

"He's in da wrong job," Brenner said. "A guy wit' an eye like that, he shoulda been bombin' Tokyo."

We inflated the raft and started paddling our way forward again. We'd gone only about twenty feet, though, when the raft started to sink; it had a hole in it. We beached the thing on a mud bar, and luckily there was a repair kit in a little pocket in the boat. Brenner fixed the hole and we were off again, and again it sank—another hole.

"Of all the blasted luck," I cried. "We'll never reach that boy if the breaks don't start falling our way for a change."

"Take it easy, boss. I'll have this one fixed in a jiffy and then it should be smooth sailin'." He did, and we were off again, and this time the boat didn't sink.

We rounded a bend in the stream, and there was our first barrier. A tree had fallen across the water. We had to unload the boat, lift all the food and equipment over, heave the raft over, reload, and go on. All this took a lot of time, and time was one thing we had little of. This was our third day on the ground, and we still hadn't reached the chute. Then the stream became shallow again, and we had to get out and pull the boat along.

Every thirty yards or so the water flowed over long mud flats. Here the boat wouldn't float, so with mud to our knees we pulled the boat and made our way forward. We worried all the time that a root or something might punch a hole in the rubber. Then we would come to a tree piled high with brush that had been washed against it. Here we would tunnel our way through the brush, cutting from within the boat, to the tree and unload and reload again. It was the most exasperating day I think I've ever spent. When darkness came that night, we were still at it. Dock, who had come and gone several times to refuel, flew away and said he'd be back in the morning. He also told us the pleasant news that we were close to the chute.

Brenner and I pulled the boat up into elephant grass bordering the stream. We cut down some of the grass and prepared to spend the night, so tired we didn't even bother to put up the parachute tent. Our parachutes were wet through, but they were all we had, and they would have to do, this time as ground cloths and blankets. We tried to build a fire, but everything was so wet the best we could get was a little smoldering of wood and smoke, not enough to dry our parachutes. Since we couldn't cook over that flame, we ate a couple of crumbled, water-soaked crackers and lay down to get some sleep.

It looked like it was going to be another tough night: The field we were in was well stocked with rats that continually ran over our faces and hands. We tried to sleep anyway. "There's one thing about a job like this," I told Jim as I wrapped up in my damp chute, "you always get your daily exercise."

Brenner and I lay there in the dark, listening to the sounds of frogs talking the day over with each other. The high, shrill voice of an owl called in the distance, and then we heard his voice. It sounded like a roar. It sent shivers to the core of my body. It reminded me less of a cat call than anything I had ever heard, but it was. I had heard that sound before.

"Good God, what was that?" Brenner said.

"Oh, that? Just a tiger, a little closer than usual. Don't worry, he'll go away. They never come near a fire." I sounded more sure than I felt.

"Yeah, but who's got a fire?"

"I'll admit it isn't much of a fire, Jim, but I think it'll do the trick." That assurance must have satisfied him; shortly he was snoring with gusto, and soon I joined him in a duet.

What time it was, I had no idea or why I had awakened—probably a rat. I blinked my eyes against the darkness and heard Brenner's voice in a whisper, "Hey, Bill, wake up—wake up."

"O.K.," I whispered, "what's the trouble?"

"I'm glad that you told me those tigers won't come near us," he said huskily, "'cause if that's true, that ain't no tiger standing there, and I'm beginnin' to think it is."

"Where, for God's sake?"

"Right there," he whispered, pointing over my shoulder to a spot down by the stream. Sure enough, in the moonlight stood a tiger. He looked as big as an elephant and twice as dangerous. His large, evil-looking eyes seemed to be staring right at me. My hair crawled up the back of my neck, and a tingling sensation ran down my spine.

"Now if that ain't the most unnatural lookin' stump I ever seen," Brenner said. "Sure looks like a tiger, don't it?"

"That is a tiger, you fool."

"Well, whaddaya know. Maybe if I said 'boo' he'd take it on the lam?"

Jim Brenner clearly had ice water in his veins.

"Take your .45 and shoot over his head if he starts this way," I said. "I can't shoot; my gun is full of mud."

He didn't understand or he heard only the end of my sentence because the next second I nearly jumped out of my skin; the air was rent with explosions. The flash of the muzzle blast from Brenner's gun lit the surrounding area. The concussion was terrific. He was pumping lead all over the jungle. He made enough noise to scare every animal in Burma. When he was finished, there was nothing but thin air where the tiger had stood. Brenner peered into the darkness.

"Missed 'im!"

"My God, Jim! You weren't shooting *at* him, were you?"

"Why, sure. My kids in the Pacific are sending home Jap swords to the old lady. At least I coulda sent her a tiger skin."

Two sons in the Army, and he's not too old to take a chance on wounding a 600-pound tiger. *What a guy*, I thought.

Sleep was impossible. I lay there listening to the rats scurrying around and feeling the hard lumps of earth and roots dig into my back while I waited for dawn to come. Not true for Brenner. Hell, it wasn't five minutes before he was snoring even louder than usual.

At least the noise ought to keep that tiger away, I thought as I lay in the darkness and listened. He sounded like a cement mixer gone mad. Every once in a while a rat came running out of the grass and bounded over my body—as much to the rat's surprise as to mine.

When dawn finally arrived, Jim and I were off again. We were close, Dock had told us. Today we had to make it to that boy. "He could probably use a little help at this point," I thought as we forged ahead in the water.

Hour upon hour we paddled and pulled, brushed vicious red ants off ourselves, unloaded and reloaded, and brushed off more ants, as barrier after barrier went by. Around eleven in the morning, Dock in his liaison plane buzzed us in the creek a couple of times, so I got on the air.

"O.K., Bill, see that sort of overgrown path or something off to your left?" There was a barely perceptible path leading off into the jungle, which we would certainly have passed if Dock hadn't spotted it from the air. "Park your barge and start walking. When you come to the first clearing, get back on the air again, and I'll direct you from there to the chute."

The sarge and I started down the little overgrown path. It was probably an old combat trail. Either the Japs or the Chinese had used it once long ago. In some spots they'd carved directions on the trees. It was Oriental writing, but which one of the languages it was, we couldn't tell, not knowing either. Here and there we'd stumble into an old foxhole or a machine gun emplacement. In fact, there had been a battle out in this God-forsaken hole in the jungle. Around us were mortar craters all overgrown and housing frogs or snakes. Rounding a bend in the trail, we came to the first of what might be called a clearing. It was nothing more than a spot in the jungle where elephants came to wallow in the mud. I thought this must be the place Dock had seen from the air, so I turned on the radio and called him while Jim laid out a muddy, beaten up white cloth to make it easier for Dock to see us.

"Right," said Dock. "I've got you. Now start cutting about a hundred and sixty degrees. While you cut, I'll fly back and forth from where you are now to the chute. If you can stay under me, you should be able to find him, or at least his chute."

"So many directions from the pilot," I said to Brenner as we started to cut our way into the heavy brush. "Maybe he'd like to tell us what to have for dinner."

The plane droned back and forth overhead, and we cut under its course, one eye on it and one eye on the compass needle. It was still slow going, but we were gradually getting closer to our objective, and our excitement increased with every step.

"There it is, Bill, up there," Brenner yelled, pointing up into a tree ahead of us.

"My God, you're right, Jim. Let's go," and we started cutting at an even faster pace.

Suddenly we stopped. We didn't have to go any farther—we knew. We couldn't see anything but the chute in the top of the tree, but we could smell it. The odor of decaying flesh permeated the area around us.

"I'm sorry to say, we've found the boy and he's dead," I radioed.

"That's tough," Dock replied. "Get all the dope about the whys and wherefores, and I'll let you know tomorrow what the major wants you to do."

"Tell Hedrick for us that, if he wants this boy's body brought out, he'll have to send Graves Registration in to get it because neither Brenner or I will do it. The body is too far gone even to get near it with a full stomach, if you see what I mean."

15

We stood there in the jungle stillness and looked at each other, each awfully glad of the comfort it gave us to have the other there. Deep in the heart of this jungle, miles from any type of civilization, with no company but a decaying body was not my idea of comfort.

"Well, Jim, shall we go and see what happened to the kid?"

"I can stand it if you can."

Slowly and reluctantly, we cut our way over to the chute. What we saw was the most horrible sight I think I've ever seen, and it will be forever embedded in my memory.

"He's been dead at least ten days," Brenner offered in a low voice, his face working. He'd been thinking the same thing I had: Would we have been able to save the boy's life if we'd been faster and cleverer on the trail? I counted back and thought not; he was probably dead the day we jumped. If we had landed right beside him we wouldn't have been able to do him any good.

What puzzled us as we stood there and looked at him was why he had died. From what we saw, there didn't seem to be any logical reasons for the whole setup. But as we looked closer we could picture all that had happened.

He had come down in a tree. It was a small tree, but his chute had caught in the upper branches and allowed him to drop through. He had ended up sitting in his parachute seat about six feet off the ground. Normally that would be a perfect tree landing. He hadn't hit limbs on his way through, at least not hard enough to break any. Sitting there so close to the ground, he had unbuckled his chest strap first, then his right leg strap. Before he could unbuckle his left leg strap, he had obviously lost his balance and fell forward out of the seat. The left leg strap slid up his leg, or down, as the case may be, and wrapped around his left ankle. This left him hanging upside down, one foot caught in the strap and his head on the ground.

This was all guesswork, but there seemed no other way for him to become caught in that position. Even then he might have been able to extract himself, but there were the ants. They must have started to crawl up his face almost immediately.

The kid used his head. He evidently had lost his knife in the bailout since it was nowhere to be found. Without a knife, there was only one way he could possibly get his foot out of that snare: shoot the strap off, which he tried. When we found him only an eighth of an inch of strap was left holding his foot. He must have run out of shells. Hanging there with ants chewing on his face, probably running into his eyes, up his nose, and into his mouth and at the same time shooting at a strap wrapped around his foot was no mean feat, yet he almost made it.

He did save one shell, though. When the ants became too numerous and the end became inevitable, rather than die an excruciating death in the claws of those big ants, he used that last shell. The hole was there for us to see.

There was nothing for us to do. We couldn't help him now. We couldn't have helped at any time. He probably died within hours of leaving his ship. We stood there, trying to understand, then turned and made our way back to the elephant wallow for the night.

We lay there under our parachute tent, surrounded by dense fog and the smell of death. We spoke little. I stared into the fire and thought of all the years that kid had spent growing up, going to school, coming home at noon for lunch. His mother met him with a white apron in the kitchen, and he hurriedly gobbled down his food so he could meet the gang. I thought, too, of the dog that had missed him when he left for the Army and now would never see him again. There were also the spankings his dad had given him and the fun they had when they went fishing. All that to end with his dead body hanging by its foot like so much beef in a butcher shop, his skull picked clean by the ants, lying there to one side, grinning at us in horrible disbelief, the buzz of flies and the masses of ants running over what remained of this fine, strong boy. An eighth of an inch of cord stood between him and his struggle for life.

The odor of death surrounded us that night. Jim pulled out his old mouth organ and softly played a few patriotic hymns that reminded me that we all took chances. The music eased the pain. Sometimes we are lucky, and sometimes we aren't. A life is a hell of a lot to give for your country, but then it's a hell of a country.

Dawn never came; it simply grew lighter. We ate a little breakfast and waited for Dock. At nine o'clock, we heard his engines.

"The major," he said, "directs you to collect the dog tags and bury the body, making certain to plainly mark the grave so that later Graves Registration can come in and exhume it for a proper burial in an American cemetery."

"Right, but what do you want us to dig the grave with, our fingernails?"

"No, I have a small entrenching shovel all ready for you and here it comes."

The plane flew right over the top of our tiny clearing, and a shovel came hurtling down at us. Again we ran like hell into the jungle to escape being hit. We stood there puffing, and Brenner, looking disgusted, said, "Why don't those guys just use a bomb and get it over with? I'm sick of having everything from hundred pound boxes to shovels thrown at me."

We made our way back to the body. Near where he hung we hacked a small clearing out of the jungle and dug a hole. It was difficult work as the ground was full of roots. We remembered a grave is supposed to be six feet deep; I wish we hadn't remembered!

We built a light bamboo litter and cut the body down from its perch onto the litter. We had no gloves or masks, and it was a gruesome business. The ants, time after time, attacked us, and the flies buzzed from the decaying flesh to our faces and lips. We got the body down into the grave, but not the head, which the ants had separated completely. It seemed inappropriate to kick or push it into the hole, and picking it up with our bare hands was out of the question. Jim, with two sticks, solved the problem.

After that, we filled in the grave, covering it with white jungle flowers. At its head, we mounted a crude bamboo cross and hung one dog tag on it for identification. We didn't know what to do next, so over the grave we fired our .45s in a salute to the soldier. Then, with flies buzzing around and the ants thinking we were more to eat, we said a few words resembling prayers, among which we included words that somehow this needless waste of boyhood would cease. It was questionable how much good these prayers would do, but it was worth a try.

Dock was still flying around, so when we got back to the clearing I radioed up. "Dock, how the hell do we get out of this country?"

"You've been working your way closer to civilization all the time. Just follow that river you were on until you come to a torn-down bridge. Stay there, and I'll get a truck to work its way down that old abandoned road to get you."

"How far is it?"

"By air it's about ten miles, but then you can't fly, can you? Ho, ho!"

"Ho, ho, yourself, birdman. Let us out of here, and one Dock Hudson better take off in high gear for that and sundry remarks made in the past."

"Negative, negative. You'll be too tired. It's about twenty-five or thirty miles to where you meet the truck, at least by the river route. And, may I add, the water looks awfully wet."

"Nuts, Hudson," I said. "The sarge and I will be there tonight waiting for your truck to show up. These are men at work down here, little boy."

"Work, yes, but men, negative! From up here all I can see are a couple of babes in the woods."

We were on our way back to the boat, so we ignored him. Walking along, I said to Jim, "Fine friends we have, always giving the helpful hand. I'm glad we have a sense of humor."

The hike out of that country was nothing to sneeze at; we unloaded that boat and loaded it so many times I felt like a dock hand at the San Francisco shipyards. Most of the time we pulled it, knee deep in mud, but we couldn't leave it behind as some day we might need it again. Also there were still the deep spots in the river that would have been impossible to walk through. That river twisted and turned all over Burma. It made horseshoe and hairpin turns back and forth until we became dizzy. Walking for two or three days in water, pulling a rubber boat loaded down with equipment, builds beautiful blisters on hands and feet.

It was late at night when we finally reached our destination, the torn-down bridge. Before we got there, though, we'd begun to look for places to sleep along the riverbank. Walking in water at night in that country isn't conducive to a long life—too many snakes that can't be seen. Just about the time we were ready to give up for the day, we heard a faint "Hallo-o-o."

We answered and in a few minutes saw a light being flashed down the river. We'd lost our flashlight in one of the unloadings along the way so all we could do was continue yelling at them, whoever they were. At that point we didn't care; anyone out in that wilderness would look good to us.

Dock, as good as his word, had flown to an airstrip and dispatched a truck to pick us up. Hot coffee was ready and good hot food. Ten minutes after eating, the sarge and I were asleep in the back of a bouncing truck.

16

The sight of so much mail when we got back to the base was a treat. Since we'd been gone, the outfit had changed locations, and we were now living in tents. My new tent-mate, I found, was Captain Owen Sutherland from Los Angeles, California. While we'd been in the jungle, a liquor ration of one bottle of whiskey had been issued. He had bought mine for me and saved it. Also I was due a case of beer. It was almost too much, coming all at one time. In the pile of mail waiting for us were also a couple of packages from my wife containing shrimp, sardines, liquor, and hors d'oeuvres—it was a cocktail party in the making!

The sarge and I showered and dressed in our new shorts—a new issue from the Army, which was apparently taking lessons from the jungle-savvy British. We sat around the tent reading our mail, eating sardines, and drinking puddlers highballs. To the uninformed, a puddlers highball is a shot of whiskey followed by a drink of beer. Or, as the sarge put it, "a slug of da' hard stuff and a swig of hot brew." That drink has put stronger men away than Jim and me.

By five o'clock the night we arrived back, Jim and I were stinking. The whiskey had gone down the drain, and the beer was waging a losing battle. People kept dropping in all day, and if they weren't flying they would sit around awhile and have a few and just generally shoot the bull. It was very pleasant and friendly, and we were getting drunker by the minute.

Jim read us something someone had written him, and then I'd read something somebody had written me, and we laughed—it didn't have to be funny, we just felt good and were glad to be out of the jungle.

The air was filled with good fellowship and the smell of sardines. We met a new member of our team, Captain Austin Lamberts of Delevan, Wisconsin, who we immediately nicknamed Doc because he was the flight surgeon of the unit. He had training as a paratrooper as well, an unheard of combination. If we needed a doctor in the jungle from now on, he would be the boy who jumped to us. Little did we realize how soon we would all have to go to work.

Captain Bill Davis came in as well as Dock Hudson, whose wisecracks had entertained us in the jungle, but all was forgiven. Later some of them told me that during our celebration that night I fired a few signal flares from a Very pistol down the length of the tent—causing everyone to dive for cover—but they probably made that up. It was midnight when the sarge staggered over to his tent and went to bed. I flopped into mine and settled back blissfully for a couple of day's rest; and while I don't recall everything that happened during our party, I do remember that I had plans to sleep for two days straight.

At five in the morning, somebody was shaking me. "Wake up, lieutenant, wake up, will ya?" the voice kept saying.

"What the hell for?" I mumbled through my beard.

"You're alerted to jump this morning, and you're supposed to be aboard the plane in an hour."

His answer brought from me the longest, most agonized groan a man can give. I put my hand to my spinning head. This was too much! How could I possibly jump this morning? Hell, I could hardly bend down to pick up my boots.

Somehow, though, I fumbled into my clothes and reeled over to the mess hall for a cup of coffee. On the way, I saw Brenner stumbling up the street; he looked awful. For a moment we stared red-eyed at each other, and then he mumbled something about "No union rules in this army."

Feeling better—not much, but better—we reported to Major Hedrick's office. If he knew what we'd been doing the night before, he gave no sign. He was all brisk and business-like. The sight of such energy was nauseating.

We each listened with one ear while he briefed us and pointed to his wall map. It had something to do with a native runner who had told somebody about someone somewhere who was lost . . . or something. It all sounded routine, but it was bewildering. We figured the flight crew would take us to the right section of country and then we could bail out and lie down in the grass or jungle or someplace and get some sleep—anywhere, just so we could sleep. After that, we could find the lost Joe, wherever he was.

The old sarge and I crawled into the plane and immediately fell asleep on the floor. When the pilots, Capt. Bill Davis and Capt. Jack Knight, came aboard, I vaguely remember one of them saying, "Would you look at those two, sleeping like babies before a picnic. You'd think bailing out of a plane is something they did every day."

"It practically is," the other one said. "I wouldn't want their job."

I think our reputation for being cool customers went up a little that day, but all I can remember was that I wanted them to go away and leave us alone.

They flew us to the airstrip where the native had made his report, a flight that fortunately took a couple of hours, allowing us to get some more shut-eye. When we landed, the native was gone, but the intelligence officer at the field had the information, such as it was. According to him, the native had come down from the north above India. We looked where he indicated on the map . . . and my eyes bulged. The area the officer pointed to contained some of the highest ranges in the Himalayas. The native had heard the story about an American ten days north of his village, and his village wasn't exactly in the heart of civilization. I figured a native could go perhaps ten miles a day on the trail in those mountains—assuming there were trails— putting our lost crew member a hundred miles from his village. My map showed that to be in Tibet.

And here I'd hoped to be home in two years, but now I could see that I might not get home at all.

Our maps indicated no villages in that territory, and all the rivers were dotted lines, which meant they were not surveyed nor were their locations certain. In other words, nobody had been up there, or if they had they'd forgotten to tell the map-makers where the rivers were. Being well north of the normal Hump flights, it wasn't the usual place for a plane to go down, but sometimes bad weather over the Hump took pilots off course, and a downed plane in Tibet wasn't out of the question. Others had gone down there before. In fact, I vaguely remembered a story of four guys who walked out of Tibet, but it had taken them a very long time.

We took off from that base and flew north, passing as we went the last trace of a settlement, a British tea plantation owned and operated by a couple named Munroe. It had been into this plantation that the native had come. The Munroes had sent him back with blankets and food and a bottle of brandy, but they had told the intelligence officer they were doubtful whether the stuff would arrive where it was needed. At least it gave Jim an incentive—a bottle of brandy lay somewhere along the route.

As we flew over their plantation, we could see it was smack on the edge of the first range of mountains. Wistfully I watched it pass beneath us.

Why couldn't we get an assignment to jump into a place like that someday? I stared moodily at the ground.

Our plane climbed constantly. The deeper we went into this country the higher the mountains rose. In the distance we could see a series of snow-capped peaks; the map showed one or two of them to be over 23,000 feet.

Maybe we should jump with oxygen masks, I thought. Where we were, though, the mountains weren't quite that high. Here they only came up a mile or a mile and a half. But they looked pretty rugged and formidable nevertheless.

"Just think, you lucky fellow," I said to Jim, "you can have the pleasure of sweating your way back over each and every one of those mountains we are passing."

"Shut up," he moaned. "I think I'm goin' to die."

Then Bill Davis called me forward and pointed off to the west. "See that piece of country over there?"

It looked about the same as the stuff we were flying over, forests and jungle and mountains, only now, as we moved to the north, the jungle was disappearing, I was happy to see.

"Yeah, I see it. What about it?"

"Well, for your information, that's Bhutan."

"And what might Bhutan be?"

"It's another country, you idiot."

It was a new one on me, and as far as I could see it didn't look like many people lived there.

By now we were circling a village, one of the few we had seen. The village was approximately a hundred miles, Bill told me, from the first village after Munroe's tea plantation. If the native was right—and if my calculations of ten miles a day held up in this country—this should be about where our airman was lost. No one came out of the huts, though.

"Just what the hell would an American be doing way out here?" I asked no one in particular. No one answered.

"I guess this is as close as we'll come to him," Bill said. "Do you and the sergeant want to go down and take a look around?"

I looked at those steep mountain slopes covered with tremendous trees—far larger than anything in the jungle—and had my doubts. "If you think, for a change, you could put us in the village, it might be worth a try. But good God, if you miss it'll take us a week just to get back up to it. That is, if we don't get hung in a tree or something."

We both studied the village. It was a little thing with a couple of long huts tucked neatly into the trees on the very top of the mountain. Despite my razzing him, I knew the way Bill had been dropping stuff to us on our last trip was excellent, and I had all the confidence in the world in his ability. I had to have. That tiny spot of a clearing represented the sum total of cleared level land as far as the eye could see. This was as rugged as any country I'd seen, and a miss here could be a catastrophe.

"O.K., Bill," I said. "Let's do it. The boy just might be down there, and if he isn't the sarge and I will find him somehow or other."

I went back to the rear of the ship and started getting into my parachute. Jim opened one eye and sat up. "Oh, man," he groaned, "here we go again."

We stood at the door watching the ground heave up and down as we flew over ridges and valleys. Bill made several passes—evidently judging his time—and passed back the alert to be ready. Then the bell rang, and we stepped out, for better or worse, though I was fearful it would probably be the latter.

After my chute jerked open, it took me a moment to get my head back on my shoulders and establish my equilibrium; by then, both Jim and I were swinging furiously back and forth. We were caught in a heavy mountain air current, tossed like bubbles in the wind. Often as not, I swung up even with the canopy, a dangerous motion because of the chance of a collapsed chute. This almost happened a couple of times, and I fell a little each time until it refilled with air. It wasn't so much parachute jumping as being thrown down a set of stairs in a barrel.

The wind, of course, carried us far beyond where we'd intended to land. It also separated us. The sarge disappeared behind one ridge, and I went crashing into the side of another. The impact knocked me silly, and when I woke up again I was practically down at the bottom. Looking up, I saw where I had crushed a path down the side of the hill as I bounced along. My head felt ready to burst, part from the rough landing, but part from the night before. What a time and place to have a hangover.

Now that I was out of the wind, the place I'd landed seemed as quiet as a cemetery at midnight. I hadn't expected a brass band, but, having become accustomed to the noises of the jungle, the silence seemed eerie. As soon as I could figure out nothing was broken, I got out of my harness, turned on the radio, and called the plane. Jack Knight answered.

"How do you feel? Are you all right?"

"Neither of those questions is relevant," I answered,

tremendously relieved to hear his voice, "and I refuse to answer without consulting my lawyer. But what have you done with my sidekick?"

"He's due east of you on your side of that other ridge."

Then Jim's voice broke in. I had forgotten he had a radio, too. "I'm over here, Bill."

"That's swell. But where the hell is 'over here'?"

"I'm directly across the valley from where you went down."

"Great. Move down to the valley floor. I think I can see a stream or a path or something down there, and I'll be down to meet you."

We both slid down from our respective mountainsides and, by shouting and shooting our guns in the air, we finally met in the forest.

"Now whadda we do?" Brenner asked.

"I'll be damned if I know. Let's hike along this stream, and see if we can find a trail." Then the plane came buzzing down the valley, and I got out the radio again. "We're both in the pink, maybe even the red, and a little raw here and there, but O.K. Where is the village we're supposed to be going to?"

"It's up on top of the ridge west of the valley you're in."

"O.K., Jack. I'd guess it'll take us most of the rest of the day and maybe more to make our way up there. You might as well go away and come back tomorrow morning. We'll try to be there when you come over."

"Right you are, boy. Sorry those mountain currents got you. There was nothing we could do. Good luck, and we'll see you in the morning."

"Detectives of the underbrush, that's what we are," I grumbled as Jim and I started wading down the stream.

17

All in full leaf and crowding each other for the sun, stalwart pines and many kinds of hardwoods covered the mountainsides and valleys. It was more like walking through the forests of Pennsylvania than the heart of Asia. Eventually Jim and I came to a well worn log stretching across the stream. At either end of the log was a trail, the trail we had been hunting for. The log was a bridge used by the natives. The trail crossed our course at a right angle and we had to make a choice: right or left. We chose left.

The trail was rocky and narrow but well trodden, and this gave us hope it might lead to the village. But the trail was used by more than natives. As we rounded one of its many twists and curves, Jim, who was in front, stopped dead and exclaimed, "My God, Bill, look at that!"

What he was looking at was also looking at us. A four-footed beast, it stood about six feet tall with broad, husky shoulders. Its hair was short with splotches of black and white, and it had short, ugly-looking horns. At first glance, it looked to be a bull mixed up slightly with the buffalo tribe. And it looked angry: Its head was lowered, and it was sniffing the air, though its sniff sounded more like a snort to us as we stood there, frozen and staring. For a moment we just looked at each other, us and the bull. Then he made up his mind and rumbled forward, his nostrils blowing up dust as he breathed close to the ground—which, of course, pointed his horns directly at us. It was like a locomotive pulling out of the station; I could almost see the fire shooting out of his nostrils. In the hundred feet or so that separated us, he picked up tremendous speed, bearing down on us, feet pounding, head lowered.

We stood frozen to the ground, hypnotized, so surprised by finding such a beast in the mountains that we couldn't move. Just in the nick of time, we both jumped to the side and into the brush as he ploughed through the air where we'd been standing. A second after he passed we scrambled out of the undergrowth and ran down the path away from him. We ran, looking over our shoulders at every step, until our lungs ached and the ground heaved under our feet. Finally, far enough away from him to be safe for a moment, we crawled into the brush and sat on a log. He had come so close I could still feel his hot breath, and the odor of his hide was still with me.

"I ain't sure whether that's real or left over from last night," Jim said, breathing hard.

"It's a good thing we didn't hang around to find out. I wonder what the hell it was and what we did to make it angry."

"All I hope is that the woods ain't filled with 'em."

After resting a little and making sure the bull hadn't followed us, we continued down the trail but with a little more caution. Soon the trail started to wend its way upward, and we felt we were on the right track at last. But we'd not gone far uphill before we got our next surprise—a native coming down the trail.

We all three stopped with a suddenness that was almost comic. Here we were in the most remote mountains I'd ever seen, and the place was crowded with animals and people! I don't know what he expected to see, but he wasn't like anything we'd ever seen before, and the surprise showed all over the three of us.

The man before us was small and fierce looking with brown skin and completely armored with bamboo. On his head he wore a small bamboo helmet, but his hair was the most surprising thing about him. It was coiled into an elongated ball jutting out from his forehead. Through this he had a long sliver of bamboo, with two cords from the helmet wrapped around the bamboo stuck in his hair. Altogether, it made a rather fearsome sight. Around his midriff were coils of bamboo, ostensibly to protect him from knife blows or spear thrusts, and around his hips and legs was a cloth skirt. Across his back was a woven bamboo shield, while on his chest in a bamboo sheath was a long knife, almost a sword. He had his hand on the hilt of that knife, and his eyes were not smiling.

For a long moment Brenner and I stood there staring; it took us that long to recover ourselves. This man looked like something from our aboriginal past. I held up one hand like I was getting ready to say "How," smiled, and said, "Glad to see you my friend. Where did you leave the rest of your army?"

He backed up the trail, slowly at first, then turned and ran up the hill.

"Maybe he don't understand English," Jim said. "Anyway, this sure doesn't seem like the land of brotherly love. Did ya see the armor plate on that guy?"

"Yeah. Maybe we ought to call for tanks and artillery. Something tells me this isn't a healthy place, or else these birds are more bashful than they look."

Still, we had our airman to find so we continued up the hill; there was little else we could do. And then yet another surprise: this time a boy about ten, dressed exactly like his elder, the same bamboo armor, the same cloth wrapped around his hips, and a cloth thrown over his shoulders like a cape. He didn't seem quite so startled, though, and just stood there looking at us, puffing moodily on a pipe as we approached.

When we were near enough I offered him a cigarette, my face all smiles and my head nodding, the very essence of friendliness. He took the cigarette, gave it a cursory glance, then tore open the paper and put the tobacco in his pipe, puffing and gazing at us like he was wondering who or what we were. Brenner and I, taking the hint from his clouds of smoke, sat down, took out cigarettes and lit them with my lighter.

That interested him. He reached for the lighter and I gave it to him. Then he and I were busy for a moment as I showed him how it worked. He liked it and, for the first time, smiled. He reached into the bag that hung around his neck and brought out a small stone and some feathery wood shavings. With these he proceeded to build a little smoldering fire by striking the stone against his knife blade and catching the spark in the shavings—the old flint and steel method. His lighter was no Ronson, but it was effective nevertheless.

Seeing that this technical and cultural exchange might be getting us someplace, I reached in my pocket and brought out a burning glass, which is nothing more than a small magnifier. I caught the sun's rays in the glass and reflected them onto his shavings and again they began to smolder, causing him surprise. He was interested, so I gave him the glass. He looked at it a minute, then handed it back, but I insisted and put it into his bag.

"When you two kids get through playin'," Brenner interrupted, "I think it's time we moved on."

"Right," I said, smiling at the boy. "But let's make a friend first before we enter the village."

The lad was studying his new possession. He looked at me through the glass and laughed at the distortion. I laughed, too, and then rubbed my stomach and made motions like I was eating. He got the idea and motioned us to follow him up the hill. This was more like it; action at last.

We climbed for quite awhile. With the appearance of first the man and then the boy, I thought the village might be near, but I began to wonder if I was wrong. What's more, the hill became steeper as we went up. We two grown men tried to stay up with the boy, but he and the altitude were too much for us; we had to stop and catch our breath. He grinned, which I took to be a good sign, as Brenner and I sat on the ground puffing like a couple of old men. After a couple of such stops we reached the top.

When we did top the crest, there was nothing there but a falling down shack and a fallen down old hut. It was definitely not the big village we'd seen from the air, merely a shelf on the mountainside with two dilapidated bamboo and wood houses perched on it. Still, in front of the house that was the least rundown a little fire was going. Logs surrounded the fire, and the boy motioned us to sit on them.

He entered the house, which like all the others I'd seen in this part of the world was built off the ground on stilts. He came back out carrying a bamboo tube filled with water and stuck the end of this in the flames.

"Tea!" Brenner said, watching him brewing the stuff. "Ugh, what we need is a drink."

"Yeah, and a new Cadillac would be nice. We've about as much chance of getting either one."

We drank the tea out of bamboo cups, and it really wasn't bad—strong and black but invigorating. As we drank we were joined by two men and a woman, the woman quite attractively dressed in black cloth. Her hair was rolled into a tight bun at the back of her neck. She had bright, clear skin and jet black hair, and her eyes had the proper amount of the exotic, but she looked like she belonged to the tough customer she came with. And he was a hard-looking egg. He was dressed as the boy and the earlier man, except in his hat he wore a huge black and white feather sticking out the rear. Of all things, around his neck on a cord he wore a large tablespoon.

Where he'd gotten a tablespoon in these mountains was impossible to guess, but it was easily his proudest possession. And since it seemed to confer something—rank, wealth—I stood up and bowed to him. He grunted as he stood there, arms folded, surveying me. I looked at the spoon and clucked my approval. He smiled his acknowledgement at my compliment of his finery. Reaching into my pocket, I brought out a Boy Scout knife, demonstrated it, and gave it to him. He thought that was pretty swell, too. From my other pocket I pulled out some five and ten cent store junk jewelry, trade goods I'd stashed earlier, picked out a red necklace, and handed it to the young gal.

Brenner and I were in solid. The big chief, all companionable now, sat down on the log by the fire. His wife, which I guessed her to be, handed him his pipe. Motioning it away, I handed him a cigarette and, taking one myself, lighted it. He got the idea and beamed his pleasure as we sat there and smoked. Hurrying natives in any way only led to mistakes, so we sat there in silence for a while.

After smoking for a bit, I pointed to myself and to Brenner and said, "American." He pointed to his chest and said "Duppla."

Well, at least we know what they call themselves, or at least what he calls himself, but who in the name of heaven ever heard of a Duppla? But I smiled and nodded as if the whole world knew of Dupplas, and it was an honor to be having tea with the president of a nation or whatever he thought he was.

By this time we'd been joined by a dozen other Duppla, both men and women. Whether they'd been hiding until they figured out we weren't going to cause trouble I don't know, but they all joined the big cheese around the fire and joined us in tea. Everything seemed to be going about right, so I tried again: I pointed off to the north and asked, "American?"

All the heads turned in my direction, and there was a stirring of conversation among them, but none of them answered my question. I tried again, this time pretending I was sick or dead. At this they all laughed, as if I was putting on a show. I'll admit, it might have looked like a ludicrous performance by a ham actor, but I was in no mood for jokes—we had important business to do. But I guess they didn't realize that and perhaps thought we'd been sent to entertain them.

As it grew dark the people began leaving in twos and threes—possibly because our acting was lousy—and we didn't get an invitation to dinner. Even the little warrior and the big cheese left, and Brenner and I were soon alone.

"Pretty sweet work," Jim grumbled. "We don't know anything more than we did before, and we ain't got nothin' in the house to eat. This is a hell of a mess."

"Jim," I whispered, and pointed to a nice fat jungle chicken all decked out in colored feathers, up by the house. Slowly Jim reached for his .45 and for the special ammo that Search and Rescue issued to pilots and aircrew. Loading the gun with bird shot cartridge, he took careful aim and fired. One shot did it, and the bird gave its all for the war effort. The patriotism may have been a little forced, but it was delicious.

The night mountain air was chilly so we built up a large fire and gathered plenty of firewood. Jim pulled out his mouth organ and started to play, of all things, "Trees." After a moment he put down the instrument and sang a parody of the poem that went, as far as I can remember, something like this:

> *I think that I shall never see*
> *A girl who'll refuse a drink that's free,*
> *A girl whose hungry eyes aren't fixed*
> *Upon the drink that's being mixed,*
> *A girl who will not wear*
> *A lot of junk to match her hair.*
> *But girls will always be loved by me,*
> *'Cause who the hell wants to kiss a tree?*

"Beautiful, Jim, beautiful. Where in the hell did you pick that up?"

"I got a million of 'em," he said. "Yes, sir, a million of 'em."

"Well, that one's enough for me. It stinks. Anyway, look who's coming."

Moving into the light of our fire was a little wizened man followed by three kids. The old boy had some sort of bamboo container under his arm, and I could swear, as I watched him approach, that he was weaving.

"Jim, are my eyes going back on me, or is that old geezer staggering, like from too much hard stuff?"

"He's plastered to the eyebrows, or me name ain't Brenner."

For a moment the old boy just stared at us, none too steadily, and then made himself comfortable before our fire while the kids hung bashfully in the background. He handed the bamboo container to me. I took it and had a swallow, then sputtered like a sick pea-shooter. It was rice wine, but wow! He must have mixed it with turpentine or something. I smiled at Jim and said, "Here, try some of this; it's about your size."

He took a swallow, and his face turned crimson. "Christ, that's hundred octane stuff," he gasped. "No wonder the old boy is weaving."

He passed the jug back to its owner and he had another drink, then passed it back to me. I drank again, scalding my tonsils, and passed it on to Jim. 'Round and 'round it went, but it was warming.

After we had killed the man's wine, we decided to retire. It had been a long day and had begun with fewer than six hours sleep, and two of those hours were on the airplane. Picking up our parachutes, we made our way into the one more-or-less intact house, laid our chutes on the floor, and rolled up in them.

"Look who's joining us," Jim said, poking me in the ribs.

Sure enough the old duffer and the kids were coming through the door apparently to spend the night with us. The little room was small, about ten feet square and a little crowded with six of us stretched out on the floor, but the old man seemed to like this as he cuddled up close . . . for the heat, I hoped.

"Boy, this guy's breath is lousy," I said to Jim. "He ought to try Listerine or something."

"You're kiddin'? Look what I got." Jim had the little girl on one side of him and the two boys on the other. It was comical; just like a whole family sharing a bed. I couldn't help laughing. "Yeah, funny. Well, at least they'll provide some warmth," he said and threw his parachute over them all and promptly went to sleep. And he was right—with six of us crowded into that tiny room, together with the hundred-proof wine in our bellies, we stayed warm through the night.

18

In the morning we woke to the sound of our search ship circling in the distance. They didn't know where we were. Shaking the sleep out of my head, I called him on the radio. "Hey, airplane driver, you're circling the wrong village. Come east, over on the next ridge."

"Just what the hell are you doing over there?" the voice of Jack Knight came back to us.

"We went where we was took by da' mob. And anyway, this little nest of fleas has a southern exposure."

"Have you found out where the missing personality is?"

"We haven't found out anything except the people are Dupplas, and that's no help. You don't happen to have a little canned chow on board, do you?"

"Sure do," he answered, "and a couple of packs, rifles, and blankets. Is there anything else you need down there?"

"Yeah, Jack, you might drop us some silver rupees, junk jewelry, small knives, mirrors, rice, and stuff like that. We're not doin' so well as things stand now."

"O.K., Bill, when do you need them?"

"Tomorrow will be swell, Jack. It doesn't look like we'll be going too far anyway."

"Right, Bill, and here's the stuff we have aboard now," he said as the plane made a pass at our parachutes, which Brenner had spread on the ground.

The dropping chutes blossomed, and our supplies came sailing down to us. Included in the drop were a hundred pounds of rice, which Brenner and I immediately opened and started dishing out to the natives. This, they thought, was a swell idea, and called all the neighbors. In an hour, we had a mob of Dupplas around us, all receiving a pound or so. We'd seen only two huts so far, so where they came from we couldn't tell, but with the rice handout matters seemed at least to be more cheerful.

Now that I had what looked like the whole village, I tried again to make them understand what we were there for, but to no avail. As in our earlier efforts, they merely thought we were being funny and laughed uproariously at our antics. We were getting nowhere but fast.

Knight was still buzzing around above us, so I called him: "Jack, where is the next village north of here? Is it far, and what's the compass bearing? We're losing valuable time with these people down here, and we might as well move on to someplace else. Maybe they'd know something about the missing victim."

"There's a village on top of the next ridge roughly north of you. The compass bearing is around three hundred degrees."

"Thanks. I think we'll try to make our way over there. See you tomorrow."

Brenner and I picked up the packs that had been dropped to us, loaded them with food, and started down a path that led north. There was more than the two of us could carry, so we left some things and took only what was necessary. The natives couldn't figure out what the hell was the matter with us and tried to make us stay. They enjoyed this free food coming from the air, but we were not to be persuaded.

After we had gone about a hundred yards, we heard the sound of footsteps on the trail behind us. We stopped and waited. It was the little old character of the previous night. He pointed to his chest in a knowing attitude, and, with a smug look on his face, pointed down the trail.

"I gottcha, brother, you're our guide," I said, "and do we ever need one in this country."

All that day we followed the old customer. He was generally going north all the time so I guessed he knew what he was doing. It was beautiful country, and a whole different kind of forest than the jungles we'd seen. It felt a lot healthier. There were no flowers of any sort—it was too cold for that—but the leaves were green and clean, and the trees were mammoth. Brenner and I measured one at its base. Its diameter was larger than both of us standing together arms outstretched. We figured it was about twelve feet through the center and 150 feet high.

Here on these mountains there wasn't the infernal tangle of the jungle's underbrush. We saw plenty of brown squirrels and some rabbits. Around three o'clock we began hunting fresh meat for dinner. We shot three squirrels and a half dozen rabbits. That may seem like an awful lot for two men to eat, but we were two very hungry men, and we had the old geezer to feed as well.

While we were sitting on a rock resting, the old man took his bow and arrow and planted an arrow in the limb of a tree about a hundred yards away. Then he turned proudly to me and pointed to the rifle I was holding. He obviously wanted me to do the same. I wonder how he thought we had been knocking off those rabbits on the fly, by mesmerism? Anyway, to satisfy the old duck, I took aim at the limb. As a matter of fact, I aimed at the little arrow he had shot up there, and, as luck would have it, I hit it. The old duffer had been sitting there with a complacent look on his face, but when I shattered that arrow his face fell six inches in disbelief. Brenner broke out into a roar of laughter at the saucer-eyed stare the old bird fixed on that limb.

"Boy," he laughed, "we won't have no trouble wit' these babies if you give 'em a demonstration like that once a week. Maybe I could sell tickets?"

"You'd better not try, Jim. That one was way over my head. After a couple of demonstrations, they'd be after your head as a crook."

"Yeah," he said, getting up, "I guess so. Come on; let's get goin'."

About five that night, we arrived at a good-sized stream with a wide bank of sand. We quickly put up a bamboo and banana leaf lean-to for the night and started cooking our day's catch. It was just becoming dark when Jim jumped up and said, "Come on, Bill, get the hell out of here—look over there!" It was one of those cow-buffalo jobs we had run into the day before.

"Wait a minute," I said. "Look what's with him!" Sure enough, the animal had a rope through its nostrils and was being led along by a little boy.

"Well, I'll be damned. He follows that kid like a puppy. Maybe this is a tame one." Behind the cow came a long line of natives—men, women, and children. They all busied themselves building fires and laying banana leaves on the ground to sleep on.

"Looks like we have company."

"Yeah," Jim said. "I hope they're friendly. Those fires could be for us."

But they weren't. These were some of the same natives we'd been with that morning, plus a few new additions. We watched them prepare their dinners. They had brought along all the rice we'd given them—about twenty-five pounds left—as well as all the equipment we hadn't been able to carry. They put it down close to our fire. Clearly they had brought it for us, returning even the rice we hadn't handed out.

"They seem like pretty nice people, Jim," I said.

"Yeah, they seem to be on our side."

As we sat there watching them, I spotted one little boy who could barely walk, his foot was so swollen. I called him over, but he was hesitant to come. The old man who had been with us all day got up, caught him, and brought him to me.

"Jim, get me that jungle medical kit. I think I can fix this kid up."

The boy's mother came over and sat down to watch, then his father and then probably his aunts and uncles. It was quite a group.

"This better be good, Bill. Ya got a tough audience watchin'."

"Well, something ought to be done. Anything would be better than the way he is now."

"Try and tell his old lady that if you mess him up."

His foot was badly infected. It was swollen up over his ankle and I could see the streaks that spelled a bad infection. In the kit was a little tube with a needle already in place that contained morphine. I stuck the needle in his foot and gave him a shot of that. It was all the anesthetic I had. It wasn't too good, but it would help a little. While I waited for the morphine to take effect, I washed his foot with warm water and soap. It was probably the first time any of them had ever even seen soap.

After the foot was bright and clean, I felt the bottom of it. At one place I felt a little hard lump. I took a razor, cleaned it with iodine, and, with Jim holding the lad's foot, I made an incision into the lump. Nothing but blood emerged.

The crowd murmured at the sight of the blood. The boy had given a yell, and there was no doubt in anyone's mind that I had hurt him. With a little prayer, I dug the blade in deeper and at the same squeezed. This time a little yellow pus flowed out of the hole. Success!

That brought a general "Ah!" from the audience. I gently pressed the wound for a while until I was certain all the pus had drained. Then I stuck a piece of gauze into the cut to hold it open and, after putting a little sulfa on it, loosely bandaged the foot. He limped away, and from there on I was in business. Native after native came up to me. One had a cut that was only slightly infected, while another had one much like the boy's. They had the usual sores, open and dangerous. There was even a woman with a goiter who wanted me to cut it off. I rubbed a little mosquito repellent on it, which seemed to satisfy her. Here an old man with gout and there a little girl with a broken arm that had healed crookedly and gave her discomfort. Soon I had treated everybody for something or other.

They settled down, noisily eating; that is, all except a few.

A little boy caught a beetle, toasted it in the coals of a fire, and ate it. His father was eating bark from the trees. Why weren't these people eating rice as their friends were doing? Then it struck me. They were the strangers who hadn't been in the village this morning when we had given out the rice. Since I had not offered them any, they were eating what they had, which wasn't much. Why they hadn't just gone ahead and helped themselves was beyond me, but these were unusual people. We called them over and gave them all rice. Soon everybody was happily eating.

"God, listen to that," Brenner murmured. "Sounds like a revival meeting or somethin'."

We had gone to bed, such as it was, and above the noise of the stream the natives had begun to chant. It was a rhythmic, rhyming sort of thing, done completely in a monotone. The white light of the moon glowed eerily down on their huddled forms against the sand. It didn't seem to bother old Brenner much, though, because in a minute the chant was joined by a deep sonorous sound; Brenner was snoring, as usual.

19

The next morning at breakfast a fine-looking middle-aged native approached us. He also had a spoon hanging around his neck as well as a large feather in his helmet. We hadn't seen him the night before, so he must have arrived with the early shift. We thought he wanted rice, so I prepared to scoop some out for him, but he held up his hand in great dignity.

He pointed to his foot and cupping his hands made motions to the effect that it was a larger foot than his normal one. I looked at his foot, but it seemed all right to me. He shook his head, pointed to his foot again, then at me, then off to the north. I pointed to myself and said, "American," then pointed off to the north also and questioned, "American?" He nodded. We were on the track at last! But what had the chief meant when he pointed to his foot? I looked at his foot again, but again he shook his head. He pointed off to the north, said, "American," then pointed to his foot and made the motions that it was swollen.

"Our friend the American out there has a swollen foot. Well, if that's all it is," I said to Jim, "we're damn lucky."

The chief agreed to take us to the American, so with much excitement Brenner and I gulped the remainder of our breakfast and gathered our stuff together.

The chief pointed out three other natives and then pointed to the north. I nodded. "O.K., chief, they can come along, too. We may need them." That was fine with him. Then he pointed to the rice and questioned me with his eyes. I wonder how the word got around in these remote areas. The natives seemed to have a way of communicating I couldn't figure out. I pointed up in the air and made with my hand like a parachute coming down. That satisfied him, and we started out.

Later that morning, around eleven, we topped a ridge. Jim and I decided this would be a perfect place to wait until our search ship came over to drop to us; anyway, we were getting tired. Those natives could really climb hills in a hurry. So we spread out our white chutes, explaining through pantomime to the chief that this is where the rice would be dropped to us. He stood there, doubtfully scanning the skies.

Jim and I sat down in the shade and relaxed. We had just taken our shoes off a couple of pairs of aching feet when the plane arrived. I got out the radio and called the pilot. He hadn't seen our panels and was flying by us. "Hey, boy, come on back here. You just flew over us."

Jack Knight answered: "O.K., Bill, now I see you. Any news today?"

"Yep. We're on the road to the boy, wherever he is. Our guide tells us he has a swollen foot, but that's all we now know about him. I can't even tell you how far away he is, but we're heading generally north all the time. Each day when you come over, fly a little farther inland, and we'll contact you on the air. Is that O.K.?"

"Right, Bill," he answered, "That'll be good. Here comes your stuff. Now is there anything special you want tomorrow?"

"No, thanks. Just be sure to give us plenty of rice. I think we're feeding the entire population of the country."

Again the white dropping chutes opened out, and down came our supplies.

"A novel way of having dinner served," I said to Brenner.

"Yeah, and unusual, too."

The remainder of the day was a downhill trek and a relief. That night we camped by the river. The natives built conical bamboo baskets and tied them in the water while Brenner and I went swimming. The water, straight from the snow-capped peaks surrounding us, was ice cold, but it felt wonderful. After we had eaten, the natives pulled in the conical baskets with the biggest load of fish I've ever seen caught in such a short time. All of them weighed more than two pounds, and one of them weighed nearly ten. It was a fisherman's paradise, to say nothing of the hunting.

Two days passed, and still we continued. If we weren't sweating our way up a mountain, we were slipping and sliding down one. At one point the natives told us to take off our shoes. We wondered why until we came to the edge of a cliff. It was vertical and without the semblance of a trail, dropping about five hundred feet. Just to peek over the edge was sufficient to make the goosebumps rise.

Brenner took a look over and pulled hastily back. "We better wear our parachutes going down this one. God, look at those rocks at the bottom; one slip and squish-finish."

How right he was, but over the side we went. Climbing down was a matter of hanging on to jutting rocks, hugging the mountainside as our feet felt blindly for another toehold. Somehow we all made it, one by one, but there were times when I had my doubts. After that, Brenner and I kept wondering how we were ever going to bring our quarry out of the country over trails like these. It seemed an impossible job.

For every mile forward, we went a mile up and a mile down. It was disheartening work. Finally the night came when the chief made a gesture like sleeping and waking up, then said, "American!" Tomorrow we would arrive at our destination.

We awoke early and were off on the trail before the sun came over the mountains. This was the day for which we had worked so hard. The natives felt our excitement and anticipation, and rest periods on the trail were less frequent and shorter. Lunch on the trail that day could hardly be called a pause. Around two o'clock we were standing on the peak of a mountain with the countryside laid out in a beautiful panorama before us. The Duppla chief pointed off to a distant mountain across the narrow valley and said, "American."

We could see a village sitting on the lower part of the ridge that formed the range. It sprawled up the ridge line, and there, the native indicated, was our man. The distance, looking out over a valley, didn't seem too great if you ignored that we had to go down the side of the range we were on, across the valley, and up the other side.

We were making our way down the mountain when we heard the Doug circling. I tried to contact it on my radio, but it was behind the mountain, and our little radio wouldn't reach that far. We continued, ignoring the persistent sound of its engines. Finally we were across the valley and mounting the last barrier when the plane flew over the ridge, and we were able to contact it.

"Jack," I called, "hang around a few minutes. We should be in the village with the victim in a half an hour."

"O.K.," he answered, "You've certainly been making good time. We never imagined you to be over on this side of the ridge already."

"We've been pushing it a little. We're just about there now. I'll call you and lay out my red blanket when we hit the village."

The red blanket, which had been dropped to us earlier, was something new for us. It stood out like a sore thumb when laid on the ground and made spotting us from the air far easier. I had noticed the Duppla chief casting a covetous eye on it during the entire trip. We had plenty of them back at the base, and if he liked it I'd give it to him when the trip was finished—if it ever was. I was beginning to wonder.

We entered the village with a great fanfare of barking dogs, screaming children, and staring natives. The chief spoke to another important-looking man, who also had a spoon around his neck, and after a minute pointed to a new, green lean-to in the center of the village.

After our rush up the hill, the sarge and I were puffing and blowing like steam engines, but we started uphill again to the little green lean-to. The front was built low, and I had to stoop to see it; all an occupant looking out might see would be the legs of passersby.

A voice came from the dark interior: "Those are the best damn lookin' legs I've ever seen. They're white. Whoopee!"

I had on shorts, and we'd found our American.

But I had heard him, not seen him. It was dark inside the hut, and my eyes, accustomed to the sun, refused to function properly. I crawled inside and almost fell over a body stretched out on a bamboo bed. "How do you feel, boy?" I asked.

"Swell," was his answer. "Have a drink. You look like you need one."

"Well, I'll be damned. Now I've seen everything. Who is rescuing who around here?"

Brenner stuck his head in. "What's goin' on around here? Did I hear somebody say somethin' about a drink?"

"This is Sergeant Brenner," I said, "and what's your name?"

"I'm Tech Sergeant Marvin Jacobs. And who are you?"

"My name is Diebold, from Search and Rescue Squadron, A.T.C. Tell me, what's the problem? Do you need a doctor?"

"I don't know, maybe I do. You'd better take a look and see what you think. It's my foot. The right one."

His foot was swollen to twice its size, and he hadn't taken his shoe off. The skin bulged over the sides of the high G.I. shoe, and the stench was terrific. It looked like an amputation job, but I said, "Hell, that's not too bad, but maybe we better have a doctor look it over, what do you think?"

"Fine, just like that. Let's have a doctor look it over. Where ya gonna get him, out of the air? Or do ya have a whole hospital outside the door?"

"Exactly, out of the air. The guy's a parachutist and he'll be here in a minute."

"My God! Ain't science wonderful?"

I stepped outside to call the plane. "He's here, and he has a pretty rough-looking foot. If you've got the doc with you, you'd better drop him. I think he's needed."

"Will do," Jack said. "We thought you might be getting close so we brought him with us today. We'll send him on down."

While the plane circled and I knew the doc was getting prepared to jump, I went back in to see Jacobs, whom we quickly nicknamed Jake. Brenner was sitting beside him, having a brandy and water.

"Where did you get that stuff?" I asked as they poured me one.

"I'll be damned if I know," Jake answered. "A native brought it and some other stuff into me yesterday. Up to that time I'd been sleeping under one of those houses with nothing but an old mailbag over me. When the villagers saw this stuff coming in they must have thought something was up and that I was a big cheese or something because they built this hut and moved me into it."

"What have you been eating?"

"Well, let's see. They gave me a couple of hard-boiled eggs, and once in a while there would be a piece of dried meat handed into me by an old lady who would come around every day and talk her head off. I didn't understand a word of it, but it was something to listen to anyway."

"Jim, whip the lad up one of your inimitable dinners, only make this one digestible."

"How da ya like that? Me, what's cooked him the best food he's had since he left home, and he cracks off like that. Whaddaya want, Jake, filet mignon, or will a little cereal be da thing?"

"Make it cereal for me," Jake ordered.

I went outside to see how things were stacking up. The radio squawked a couple of times. "We're all set to go, Bill," Jack Knight's voice came in over the set. "Keep your eyes peeled. We may miss the village."

The doc didn't drop far as he had jumped low to the hill we were on. In the center of the village stood a lone tree, and darned if the wind didn't blow him into it. He crashed through the branches and landed with a thud on the ground. The natives were all rushing for him, and so were Brenner and I.

"That one didn't look too good," Brenner panted as we ran. But Doc Austin Lamberts was in pretty fair shape. He was standing there calmly watching the native who was climbing the tree to retrieve his parachute.

"Hi!" he said. "Where's the patient?" His coolness was remarkable.

"He's over there in that hut," I said. "His foot is in pretty awful shape. I hope you brought your saw with you."

"Hum-m, that bad, eh? I'll go over and give him a hand."

Then the plane started dropping supplies, and the sky was full of parachutes.

"Here come my medical supplies," the doc said. "Can you bring them over to me as soon as possible? And I'll need some hot water, too."

"Right," we answered in unison and took off after the dropping parachutes. They landed all over the countryside, but the natives, cooperative as usual, bustled to retrieve them. The sarge and I simply stood and watched as they carried those hundred-pound sacks on their backs.

In a jiffy, Lamberts had a blood plasma bottle rigged up, and Jake was getting a new start. Brenner went about getting the natives to build a place to store all of our supplies and a place for us to sleep near Jake. I got "our" chief to build a fire and make some hot water. The doc worked over Jake for the next two hours. By that time, Jim and I were just sitting there watching and finishing off the brandy. We said a silent thanks to Mr. and Mrs. Munroe back at their plantation for the stuff. We were a couple of tired apples, and the brandy really hit the spot.

The natives, both men and women, crowded around the little building to the point where they were getting in the doc's way. We had to build a fence around the place out of bamboo and shroud lines to keep them back. The only ones allowed inside that fence were the three natives who had come with us and, of course, the chief.

The chief had a marvelous sense of humor. Brenner and I pounded our chests Tarzan-fashion and said, "Me big Chief." Since we had named him Chief, he knew we were riding him. He would laugh and pound his chest and say, "Me beeg American." Always good for a laugh was to point to one of them and say, "You American," then point to ourselves and say, "Me Duppla." It was sort of corny, but it made for better friendship. The name of one of our three men was Sing Low. I sang "Swing Low, Sweet Chariot," and he thought I was singing about him and he laughed in his embarrassment.

That night as we sat there and talked, Jake told us he'd been a passenger aboard a plane that crashed and was the only survivor. He'd been lying on the floor in the back of the ship when it hit. The next thing he remembered was being on the ground some six hundred yards away from the fuselage, and it was raining. He must have been thrown through the door in the back just as it sprung open. The next day the natives came and picked him up and brought him on a litter to this village. He had been here for two weeks.

After Jake had gone to sleep, Doc Lamberts told us he thought he'd arrived just in time. The foot was broken in a couple of places, and it would be months before he would be able to walk again—but he didn't think Jake would lose it. The three of us sat there visualizing months of sitting in this God-forsaken place waiting for Jake to be able to walk his way out of this rugged country. Considering the dangerous trails we had come over, carrying him out on a litter seemed impossible.

"Maybe they can get a helicopter or something," I suggested. "I hear the Army's got a couple somewhere in China."

"Not a chance at this altitude and distance," Doc said. "Too far, too high." He was right, and the terrain was incredibly rugged. In the moonlight I looked over the country. Hills, hills, and more hills. There wasn't enough level land around here to build a marble ring for kids. Though we might have been able to make a pad for a helicopter, any kind of an airstrip seemed out of the question. We were definitely stuck, but then we'd work on that phase of the problem when we came to it. I'd learned that much anyway over the months I'd been here: Take things as they come, one at a time.

The natives had built a large lean-to of bamboo in which we piled all our equipment. But even with our gear, there was still enough room for the three of us to stretch out and sleep. As we were getting into our improvised bed, the doc said, "Would you look at that?"

We looked where he was pointing with his flashlight and there, against one of the walls, stood his stretcher. That wasn't too unusual, but on closer inspection we saw the stretcher was attached to a pole stuck in the ground. Rather than move the stretcher, the natives had built our building around it. The stretcher was part of the wall.

In the morning, Doc gave Jake his first bath in almost a month. Jake's face had been partially burned. We had thought it dirt, Brenner and I, when we first saw his face, but after a wash job we realized it was crusted skin. Lamberts said it would turn out all right and wouldn't even be noticeable after it all healed, but Jake sitting there with that crusty skin all over his face, with his dirty and ripped clothing and his long hair and beard, made a gruesome picture. After the Doc finished, the change was radical, not only with his looks, but in his morale. Jake looked so good Brenner suggested we break a bottle of champagne over him as a christening. If we'd had a bottle of champagne to break, we'd probably have emptied it first.

As we waited for the rescue ship to come over so we could discuss the pros and cons of how to remove one Marvin Jacobs from Buffalo, New York, back to Buffalo, New York, or at least part of the way, we watched a shooting match among the natives. Some of them were using cross-bows and some the ordinary bow and arrow. They took one of our cardboard boxes that had a red circle on it and sat it about a hundred yards away. One after the other, they took cracks at it. There was much hooting and jeering among them when they missed the box, which was seldom. The red circle, though, was something different, small and hard to hit. They offered a bow and arrow to the sarge and me, and we gave it a try. I couldn't even make it near the box. Brenner was a little better, but the natives were perfect compared to us.

Then they wanted us to try our rifles. Deciding to give them a show, we loaded with tracer and the "Ahs!" that went up when they saw that streak of fire head for and into the box made us feel like magic makers. Then I gave the rifle to the chief and asked him to try his hand at it. He was thrilled to death and not a little frightened. He aimed, but he was looking over the sight instead of through it and missed pretty badly the first time. I pointed out his mistake, and after that he did a creditable job of puncturing the box. From there on, he really was a big shot with his friends. Doc said it made quite a sight, Brenner and me out there in our bare feet shooting a bow and arrow with a bunch of natives using a rifle.

When the search plane came over, Bill Davis was at the controls. I asked him to drop us two hundred silver rupees to pay off the natives who had saved Jake's life, and then we discussed our evacuation problem. As Doc had said, there was no way a helicopter could operate in this kind of country and Bill agreed.

I told Bill how impossible the trails were as far as littering a man out. Back when we were trying to figure out where our man was, we figured it would take a native at least ten days to get from the Munroe plantation to here. Since we weren't nearly as nimble as the natives, it would probably take us twice that long to get back to it, and that was only if Jake could walk. There seemed to be only one solution: build an airstrip for a hospital liaison plane. But where?

Bill's voice squawked out of the radio. "I'll fly around out here and see if I can spot a piece of land level enough to build one. Don't go anywhere; I'll be back."

Who was going to do the building? I'd never done any engineer work in my life, and neither had Brenner. Where were we to get the labor? As far as I could see, these people never worked at anything except a little corn patch here and there. And to top that off, none of us could speak their language; how were we going to tell them what we wanted done? What would we use for engineering equipment? We couldn't build an airstrip with our bare hands!

I called the chief over and motioned to him to sit down. We lit up cigarettes, and I drew a long breath and started in, "Look, chief." I pointed to the plane in the sky.

The chief smiled and said, "Oranjaj."

"O.K.," I said, "so it's an oranjaj." Then I made the motion with my hands of an oranjaj flying around and at the same time imitated the sound. The chief nodded. Then I brought my hand in a slow spiral down to the ground as in a plane landing. Again the chief nodded. I wasn't certain he really understood what I meant or was trying to humor me, but I went on. Now I had smoothed out a little runway on the ground. Into the center of this I stuck a twig. Then I imitated an airplane landing again and hitting the twig, and I said, "bang, moriee" a Duppla word meaning dead.

Time after time I imitated the landing of a plane on my simulated airstrip, each time with something wrong. I piled it with bumps and turned the plane over and said, "bang, moriee." Then I made my airfield lean too much one way, then the other, all with the same results. It took a great deal of patience on my part as well as the chief's, who had to sit and listen and try to figure out what I was driving at. But he was very patient and seemed interested. Finally, after half an hour or so of repetition, I think he caught on, for he imitated an oranjaj in flight and landed it only on a smooth field. When I put something in the field, he angrily reached out and removed it before he brought his hand in for a landing.

The sarge and Doc came over and watched curiously for a while until finally Brenner spoke up, "I think you're both nuts," then walked away.

I pointed to Jake in the hut and pretended to try and walk with a sore foot. I made it look impossible. The chief nodded. Then I pointed to Jake, said, "oranjaj," then pointed down to our simulated airstrip. Again the chief nodded. He had the idea. Now all we needed was the wherewithal and the place to build it. It all looked rather unlikely. "But, hell, we'll try anything once," I said aloud.

"Now what?" asked the doc.

20

Bill Davis returned. "I think there might be a place large and level enough just over the hill you're on, but you had better go take a look at it."

"That's fine, Bill," I said, "but what will we build it with? I think I may be able to get the labor, but we'll need more than just labor."

"You order it, Diebold, and we'll do everything in our power to get it for you. Incidentally, the major has sent an interpreter in to you. He should reach you in a couple of days. That should simplify matters a little."

"It certainly will, Bill. We'll be on the lookout for him."

"One more thing. The major wants one of you two birds to go to the wreck and bury the bodies and find out all you can about what happened. And be prepared. The plane was carrying a few passengers and there probably will be some extra bodies around."

"Will do. But tell the major he ought to make one of those trips sometime, and he wouldn't be so anxious to bury the bodies. They ought to change our name to Search and Undertakers, Inc., or Major Hedrick's Mortuary."

"I'll tell him, with pleasure," Bill said. "See you tomorrow."

I hunted up Brenner. "Jim," I said, "you and some of the natives are going over to the wreck tomorrow. I'm going over the mountain to take a look at the field Bill Davis spotted to see if it's feasible to build an airstrip there. When you're at the wreck, get any mail or personal effects that might be lying about. Have the natives bury the bodies, although I doubt if there will be much left."

"Look what I found on this geezer," Brenner said. He was holding out a man's wedding ring. "This guy must've stole it from one of da bodies."

"Well, go over tomorrow and pick up the remainder of the stuff. In the meantime I'll get hold of the chief and see what this is all about."

I called to the chief and showed him the ring, then pointed to the native Brenner had taken it from and who was still hanging around, hoping to get it back. The chief looked at the ring. I clucked my disapproval and said, "American ring." He looked puzzled, so I said, "Oranjaj, moriee American, no damn good."

He caught the idea, for he called the native over and started to give him hell. The natives gathered around and all listened and then all of them started talking to the chief at once. He got up and accompanied them down to one of the houses in the village.

Brenner and Doc and I started to get dinner.

"Jeez," Jim said, "now if we only had a spot or two of

somethin', I could mix up a mean cocktail from this fruit juice they dropped us."

"Yeah, make mine a scotch and soda, will ya, while you're at it."

"Naw," said Jim, "I think I'll have a Russian Cocktail."

"What in the hell is a Russian Cocktail?"

"You mean you ain't ever heard of a Russian Cocktail? Well, I'll be damned. It's one part gin, one part vodka, with a nice plump Russian gal to go wit it."

"I'll stick to scotch," I said.

Just then the Doc, looking very bored—which should have been a warning—spoke up. "Don't you two men know that you'll never be healthy or vigorous if you drink so much? Don't you want to grow up to be big strong men with hair on your chests?"

"Lookit who's talkin'," Jim said. "Me, I'm twice your age, and I got hair all over me, and I likes the hard stuff."

"Me, too," I chimed in, "that is, with certain modifications."

"I don't know what them are, but the hard stuff never hurt nobody."

"Ah," the Doc sighed, "I give up. I guess I've run into a team of incorrigibles, but since you both seem to be such healthy incorrigibles, I've got a surprise for you." He reached deep into one of his kits and brought out a bottle of bourbon. "Jungle Ration. You two don't get much fun out here, so I brought you this."

"Now how in the hell did that get past my nose?" yelped Brenner. "I can usually smell a drink a mile away."

"What'll it be men?" I said, snatching the bottle out

of the doc's hand. "Bourbon and water, or bourbon and fruit juice?"

"Make mine straight," Brenner said. "Man-size. I'm dry as hell."

"Skip me," said the doc.

"Better have some now, Doc. I've watched these things empty before when Brenner is around."

Thanks to Lamberts, it was a beautiful night with three or four moons shining overhead. We sat around and talked and sipped. We traveled to New Guinea, the West Indies, France, Australia; the world was ours, and we were its masters. But we had some big work ahead of us in the next forty-eight hours, so we finally kicked off our boots, turned over, and went to sleep.

Early the next morning, Brenner and four natives started for the wreck. The chief, four men, and I started over the hill to look for the field Davis had reported. Before we left, though, the chief handed over a couple of pairs of dog tags, pictures of men's families, a wristwatch, and some jewelry. He had been out collecting from the natives.

The pictures affected us most. On one side of one in a double frame was the photo of a beautiful young girl and on the other a small, sweet baby. When I thought of those two receiving the telegram with the star on it because of the identification reports we'd have to turn in, my mood plummeted. We would have liked to have saved them all, and we would have if the opportunity had been given us. But they were already dead and out of our reach.

"Don't let it get you, kid," Brenner said, sensing my

depression. "When your number's up, all the struggling in the world won't help you."

He was right, but it didn't make me feel any better about this death and war business. It was all so damn useless.

The two scouting parties started out together up the remainder of the mountain. At the top, we separated. The crashed aircraft was off to the east, and our direction was west. At the parting we shook hands and looked mournful, as if we'd never see each other again. Those pictures had affected us more than we realized.

For the next two hours the going was easy, all downhill, and we made good time. The leeches and ticks were bad in this part of the country, though, I discovered. On the trail we met some natives. A few women in the party had their own answer to the nylon shortage. Actually it was to protect their bare legs from the ticks, but American women, take note: They had wrapped around their legs large green leaves. It was most attractive! When I first glimpsed them, I thought I was seeing things: green stockings in the jungle.

It was about two in the afternoon when our party emerged from the jungle onto a shelf on the mountainside. Looking down I had a bird's-eye view of the field below me. It was the only level piece of ground in view. But my heart sank when I saw it. The field was covered with stumps. The natives in this country cut down the trees, leaving the trees on the ground and the stumps standing. Around all this debris, they plant their corn and some rice. This was evidently a cornfield. It was completely covered over with the remains of last year's crop. Added to this, of course, were the fallen trees and the myriad of stumps. To make matters even worse, the field was short and completely surrounded by tall, thick-trunked trees. At either end of the field flowed a river. It was the same river at both ends; it merely made a twist to allow for our more or less level spot.

Moreover, the entire valley was surrounded by high peaks. The valley and flat area was so narrow that as I stood there surveying it, I wondered if a light plane could come down into it and circle for a landing. The only possibility might be for a plane to skim the treetops over a saddle that connected two high peaks and then, cutting the engine, drop onto the field. Taking off again would be another matter.

The whole thing looked pretty difficult, not only to build but to use as a strip. It would take hundreds of men to lift those heavy trees from the field and thousands of sticks of dynamite to blow out those hundreds of stumps. Then all the trees at each end of the field would have to be chopped down. Not just the first few, but practically the whole forest in the valley; a plane needs plenty of space to climb after it's cleared the runway. Then, somehow, we would need to smooth the bumps out of the field and fill all the holes left by the stumps. It would be quite a job and, when finished, it would be problematical whether a plane could make it in and out again successfully.

But then what had we to lose? We had to wait anyway until Jake's foot was better before we could walk him out. We could go ahead and try to build the airstrip, and if it failed by that time he should be ready to walk. If it didn't, then none of us would have to make that long hard journey out. It was worth the old try.

I nodded to the chief that I thought this was the place. He looked at me as if I were crazy, and I think I was. But we continued down the hill to the field. From above, I had underestimated the size of the fallen trees that were interlaced all over the ground. Some of those babies were six feet thick and a hundred feet long, lying on top of one another in a crazy pattern of tangled wood.

I sent the chief back for the doc and Jake—we had agreed we'd all move here if this was where we were going to work—and had the other four men start building a lean-to for Jake and for our equipment. About this time, Bill Davis flew over and I contacted him. I had to give our support guys credit; they always showed up when we needed them.

"Maybe it can be done," I told him, "if you drop us enough of the right stuff and I can get enough labor."

"We'll get you everything we can, Bill, but don't ask for a bulldozer."

"It's going to cost a lot of money. These natives have a hankering for our silver, and airports don't come cheap this year."

"That's all right, too," he said. "Any amount you need, just ask for it. The major says we need to do it."

"Right. Well, here's my first order: a dozen pick-axes, a dozen axes, a half-dozen cross-cut saws, a dozen shovels, and five cases of dynamite. Also, you had better drop me about two hundred more rupees."

"Will do. And of course you want G.I. rations and some more rice, is that right?"

"Keerect, and salt and sugar."

"O.K., we'll have that stuff as soon as possible for you. And good luck, old man, you're now an engineer."

"Strictly embryonic, and that's a compliment to my abilities."

After the plane had gone, I took one of the natives off the lean-to job and, using some pretty complicated sign language, instructed him to go to all the nearby villages and tell the people to come and help me and I would feed them and their families and pay them in silver—men, women, and children. When the lean-to job was completed, I sent the other three out with the same information and then sat back and waited. *Wait'll the old sarge sees this mess of work*, I thought. *He'll blow his top.*

It wasn't an hour before the people started to arrive. What they found must have been disappointing. There was only me sitting there, no food, no silver, no nothing. Whole families came and stood around and stared at me. I made friendly overtures as best I could. The little children hid behind their mother's skirts at the sight of this pale-skinned one and the mongrel dogs sniffed the air about me suspiciously. After quite a crowd had gathered, I spotted one of my own men, Sing Low. I made signs to tell him that tomorrow the plane would come and bring the food and silver. He told them, but they eyed me in evident distrust.

While they all stood around talking the situation over, I went out into the field and began lighting fires in the old, dried-up cornstalks and grass. The kids took an interest, and I soon had a little gang of the vagabonds running all over the place with thatches of burning grass in their hands setting fire to the entire field. Together, the little arsonists and I had it burning briskly in a matter of minutes. The wind swept the fire along over the field at a great clip, and some of the old dead logs that hadn't been too water-soaked started to burn. The fire swept up the mountain, cleaning out the brush, and, surprise of all surprises, down the side of the mountain came the animals.

At first I was too astounded to do anything but watch. There were deer, rabbits, squirrels, and even wild boar. I soon recovered myself, though, and taking my rifle I started to blaze away. The natives fell back at the sound of gunfire but soon caught on, and they, too, seeing a whole week of full bellies passing in front of them, took up their bows and arrows. It was a hunter's utopia. The animals streamed out of the woods and into the river. I braced the rifle on a stump and never had to move it an inch. A boar came into the sights, and I fired. He went crashing and kicking to the ground, and a deer popped into the sight ring, and again I'd fire. Arrows from the natives were pouring into the mass of animals like rain. Even the little children with their tiny bows were pumping them into the stream of animals as fast as they could.

When the stream finally ended, our proposed airfield looked like a slaughterhouse. The river was running red. I walked from animal to animal, shoving it with my foot. If it wasn't dead, I furnished the coup de grace with a blow from my rifle butt. The natives went around and happily collected the various animals. I made no attempt to count them all, but I'm certain there were more than a hundred small barking deer killed as well as at least fifty wild boars. These poor starving natives living in the midst of plenty would definitely eat that night and many nights thereafter. I think they imagined my getting the animals out of the woods was part of the plan, and they seemed thankful for it.

Soon fires were being built and spits put up. I made certain there was no wastage of the meat. It was all butchered that night. But I was amazed at the passage of time. It was becoming dark. Those animals had been running out of the woods for almost two hours. A couple of small panthers had been shot as well as a few monkeys. One of the baby monkeys whose mother had been shot, I rescued, and he became my constant companion. I named him Chief—another way to ride the real chief when he returned the next day with Jake and Doc.

Some of the meat was cooked that night for food. Some of it was smoked over the fires, and some of it was put in a stone-lined pit dug near the river's edge. It was the natives' version of an icebox. I had my doubts as to how long it would keep in such an arrangement, so I was surprised that it was still unspoiled at the end of a week.

In the dark, I walked from fire to fire, from family to family. At one fire they handed me a piece of deer meat. At another it was pork, and at yet another I could have rabbit. By nine o'clock I was so full I could hardly walk about. But there seemed no such limit for the natives; they ate and ate. The little children had firm round tummies for the first time in their lives, I guessed. It was all very merry, and I was happy in the thought that from now on these natives were my friends due to an accident over which I had no control.

But I had won their respect, and the chances of a successful airfield construction increased 100 percent.

Even so, the next morning I had a difficult time getting the natives to go to work. I gathered them around with the help of Sing Low and, through him, had them understand I would pay all the men two rupees a day (about sixty cents American) and the women and children one rupee per day. But, I tried to explain, this was for an eight-hour day. From eight to four or from nine to five, and I had the sun as a clock. They, of course, couldn't tell time, but, by pointing to the sun at its different positions, they understood what I meant. While they may have understood, they were, to say the least, reluctant to go to work. Organized work, especially for someone else and for pay, was something they didn't know much about.

By late morning I had the women on their knees cutting grass with their knives and the little children running around playing and sometimes carrying the grass away. The men were heaving the timbers they could lift off to one side of the proposed runway. Being the boss wasn't easy: There was more talking and sitting around than there was work being done. When I walked up to one group, they would be working, but as soon as I turned my back, they'd all sit down and talk the whole thing over. Little naked brown-skinned boys and girls were running back and forth and screaming at each other while the mongrel dogs barked. No labor foreman ever had such an assembly. I tried to count heads so Uncle Sam wouldn't take too great a beating at payoff time, but there were so many of them, and they moved about so much, that counting them was impossible, so I finally gave up. None of them had ever heard of the union rule for a lunch hour, though, so I had no trouble at noontime; they went right on loafing with a little work thrown in on the side.

That night neither the chief nor the Doc showed up. Worse, neither did Bill Davis in the plane. Here I had about 250 natives all lined up at five o'clock with their hands out and no funds. I grabbed Sing Low by the arm and told him to tell them the weather had made the oranjaj stay in bed that day. This was done through a series of mouth noises, imitating an airplane and by pointing to the clouds, closing my eyes, and walking around as if I didn't know where I was going and was lost. It was all done at the same time, and he must have grasped the idea for he turned to my laborers and talked for a few minutes. A general murmur went through the crowd. I held my breath. If they got nasty about the thing, I was helpless with so many.

Some old woman who had done nothing but sit around and talk all day came up and gave me quite a lecture, none of which I could understand, but, from the tone of her voice and the finger she shook under my nose, I gathered she didn't like the whole setup. I patted her on the back and smiled, but that didn't mollify her in the least; she went right on screaming at me. Finally I put my fingers in my ears and got down on my knees, and with arms raised over my head I did an imitation of the Moslem Salaam to Mohammed, laughing while I did it. This act drew a roar of laughter from the crowd and, completing my ham acting, I arose and kissed her on both of her dirty cheeks. I'd swear she blushed, but she did stop her infernal yelling. These natives had a marvelous sense of humor, and they were on my side because of the antics. Evidently they decided to believe me because they went about cooking their dinners. I praised the Lord for the animal hunt of yesterday, for without those animals we would have had no food as well as no money.

That night I sang them a couple of verses of "Old McDonald," and it was so lousy we all went to sleep early.

The next day, another fifty natives augmented my labor force. How I was going to be able to tell whom I owed for two days labor and whom I owed for one day was a problem I didn't like to think about. Also, two hundred rupees weren't going to be half as much as I needed. But we'd figure that one out when we came to it; right now we had work to do.

The strip was beginning to take shape. All the way up the part that was to be the runway, piles of logs and grass bordered its boundaries. There was a slightly noticeable clearness about the center in a straight line up the field. Of course, it was all still littered with stumps and trees too heavy to lift. I put everyone to work digging down to the roots of the smaller stumps and cutting them off under the ground. It was slow work, slower than if we were using dynamite, but then we had no dynamite.

At last, around ten o'clock, Bill Davis flew over, and while the natives crowded around me watching in awe I talked to the oranjaj through the little box in my hand. He had all the stuff I had ordered, and, break of all breaks, he had brought along four hundred rupees instead of two hundred, and did I need them!

Again the sky filled with white chutes as the stuff came drifting down. Rice, engineering equipment, more food, more medical supplies, clothing, tents, cigarettes, loose tobacco for the native pipes, junk jewelry, corncob pipes. Some of the rice was dropped without parachute and the bags broke. So we were not only clearing the fields for these natives, but we were planting next year's crop for them as well by scattering rice all over the field. In the middle of the drops I heard Doc's voice on the radio. He was watching the drops up on the shelf of the mountain where I had first seen the field.

"The next drop is the caps for the dynamite," Bill said. "For God's sake, be careful of those things. I'm told they'll go off from the heat of your hand, let alone a drop like this. Then after the caps comes the dynamite."

"O.K. Did you include any directions with the dynamite? I've never used any before."

"My God, no! You mean you can't use the stuff?"

"I didn't say that. I said we hadn't used any before. There isn't anything we can't do. It's just that we may need a few instructions or something."

"Good Lord, Diebold. Don't touch the stuff then until I can get an engineer to write down how it should be used."

"Don't worry, you can count on that, but we'll need those directions soon. I want to start blasting this afternoon."

"O.K., I'll have those directions for you at one o'clock."

The caps landed without incident, and I let them lie where they were until I knew how to handle them. As my work crew rounded up the scattered parachutes and packs, Doc and a whole procession of natives came across the field. They had Jake on a litter, and Brenner was with them. It was good to see them again even after such a short time. Not having anyone to talk to is the hardest part of being alone with a bunch of natives; I liked them well enough, but sometimes I just needed to talk without using sign language.

With all the excitement, I had a hard time trying to get the natives back to work, but the chief took over and was soon doing me out of a job. He ranted and raged, and in a few minutes everyone was back to clearing the field with a fervor that I'd not been able to produce with all my cajoling and pleading.

I brought Brenner up to date, and he and I started opening all the parachute bags. First we found the saws, which I gave to the chief. We started to demonstrate how to use a saw, but the chief was indignant and waved away our efforts; either he figured it out on his own, or he had used a saw before. We had him send six men out to attack the trees at one end of the runway. Next we gave him the dozen axes, and twelve men started hacking at the fallen trees on the runway. There were no shovels.

"That's a hell of a thing," said Brenner. "How we gonna build an airport without shovels?"

"You've got me, Sarge. But we always have our fingernails."

"Yeah, but we won't have 'em long if we gotta claw this thing out of the ground."

The sound of axes hitting wood and saws rasping against trees was music to my ears. Brenner and I went around with the chief from stump to stump. On the ones we would blast out, we made a knife cut and said, "boom." The chief didn't quite understand all this boom business, but he knew to leave those alone. With the little stumps the natives took the pick-axes and dug at the roots under the ground and, after baring them, chopped them off and hauled the stump away.

Still there were too many natives sitting around not doing anything. It was hard on the morale of the ones really working. I figured we had too many and that thirty could do the work these three hundred were doing. It was worth a try anyway, so I told the chief that the next morning I wanted only thirty men, no women, no children. I'd feed them all if they wanted to stick around, but no rupees. Surprisingly enough, he, too, thought this a good idea. At this point our field was cluttered up with humanity, all talking at once. It sounded like the Pennsylvania Station in New York.

That night the payoff finally came, and what a mess. To some women and children I owed two rupees for two day's work, and to others I only owed one rupee. To some men I owed four rupees for two day's work and to others only two for one day's work. I had the chief form them into groups. Everyone seemed to want to be in the four rupee group and in lesser degrees down to the one rupee group, which was almost empty. I couldn't call them liars; I didn't really know who should be where.

There was much argument and jostling around. I tried to stand aloof from all the excitement but found it almost impossible as they would come and appeal to me in a language I couldn't understand. Finally it all quieted down a little with most of them in the four rupee group except the women and children who all seemed to be in the two rupee group. There were a few sad sacks in the one rupee group, but they were in the minority.

Then I started to pay off. By the time I got to the two rupee group, all the ones I had paid in the four rupee group were trying to get into the two rupee group, but the chief sorted most of them out. In the beginning there were only a very few in the one rupee group, but by the time I got around to paying them off, the group had grown. If there was one native in the bunch that didn't make at least six rupees, he just wasn't fast enough going from group to group, that's all. I was happy when it was all over and a little grayer at the temples.

Bill Davis had dropped the dynamite instructions, but it was only now that Brenner and I had time to read them. It was a typewritten sheet with every other line typed in red letters. It was so full of warnings it frightened us to read it. We opened a case of dynamite while the doc got all set for some ready business. The dynamite was in little cans with a small hole in the top. Then we opened the box of caps.

They were two-inch long, seemingly hollow cylinders. A box of a hundred was about twice the size of a package of cigarettes. It was about these that most of the red lettering in the instructions spoke: "Don't hold them in your hand as the heat will fire them off." "Don't allow them to lie in the sun as again the heat, etc." "Don't drop them as they will certainly go off, etc." To say that we handled them gingerly would be an understatement. We didn't breathe when the box was opened.

There was also some coiled stuff that looked like wire. This, our letter informed us, was the fuse. Then there was a gadget that went on one end of the fuse. It had a tiny handle that, when pulled, lit the fuse. The other end of the fuse went into the hollow end of the cap. The end of the cap had to be crimped to hold the fuse in, but not more than three-eighths of an inch from the end. Then the cap went into the hole in the block of dynamite.

The sarge and I carefully put the whole mess together. The fuse was supposed to burn an inch a minute; we cut a six-inch fuse, pulled the handle on the lighter, and ran like hell. We sat down behind a log and waited, fingers in our ears—and we waited fifteen minutes, but it didn't go off.

"Musta' done somethin' wrong," Brenner said laconically. "Best I go take a gander at it."

"Negative. We'll both go; we both set it."

We crept up on that charge, and the closer we came to it the more certain I became that it was going to go off.

"Boy," said Brenner, "you can change me under drawers when this is over."

"Yeah, if the dynamite doesn't do it for you."

But it didn't, and we made a final dash, pulling out the cap on the fly. The lighter hadn't lit the fuse! We tried again. This time it worked. The blast created a considerable sensation among the natives who had hung around, and we were all set for the morning.

21

The chief had his thirty men hard at work at eight the next morning. He kept them down at one end of the runway while the sarge and I started blasting at the other.

Now the sound of trees falling and saws cutting was augmented by the sound of dynamite booming. Brenner and I picked out a couple of good-sized stumps and, with our hands, tunneled under it. Into this tunnel we rammed dynamite. Then, when both of our charges were ready, we pulled the lighters in unison and ran.

The results of the blasts were discouraging. These had been large trees. Their roots were thick and bore down deep into the earth. Also, the ground was of a sandy nature, and all the dynamite seemed to do was to blow the earth away from the roots. This left the tree stump still standing with a near hole at its base in which all the roots were exposed. When the roots were over two feet thick, we'd put charges under the roots in the hole previously blown. This usually worked, blowing the root in half and freeing the stump. With the smaller stumps we left the roots exposed for the natives to cut with their axes. In the case of stumps that were only three feet thick, we were able to blow those neatly out of the ground, leaving nothing but a smoking hole. One of these smaller stumps flew high in the air and landed in the middle of a fire where natives were making tea. They didn't seem to realize the danger of a chunk of tree almost hitting them, but they were very irate about our spilling their partially brewed tea.

After Brenner and I became a little more adept at setting the charges, we started setting up to ten apiece and at a signal start running from stump to stump pulling lighters as fast as we could. By the time we hit the last charge, the first one would be going off. When this happened we'd run down the field amidst a shower of gravel, dirt, and wood chips. Once, Jim was knocked flat on his back by a piece of flying log. "Jeez," he exclaimed, "ain't it great! Just like combat!"

Bill Davis flew over that day and asked, "Which end of your airfield has the firmest ground, Bill?"

Brenner and I had completed setting a dozen fuses in stumps at the west end of the field and decided to give Bill a show. "Wait a sec, Bill," I said over the radio. We ran like the wind and pulled them all, then I said: "The west end, Bill." I had no sooner said it than the charges began to go off. It must have looked like we blew a hole in the ground a hundred yards wide and deep.

Davis came back: "The west end, my eyebrow! That's the first time a runway ever came up to meet me in the air."

"Well, I just wanted you to see for yourself, so I sent it up to you for closer inspection."

"I'm gettin' out of here before you two guys shoot me down!"

Before he left, I ordered ten more cases of dynamite. Instead of spending the time sawing those trees lying on the ground, we were going to blast them into pieces the natives could carry. In turn, he had given us some bad news. He hadn't been able to find us shovels anywhere. We had to build a runway without shovels. Accomplishing that would be a first in anybody's history book.

Days passed, and Jake's condition rapidly improved. We'd been dropped penicillin, and the doc kept it fresh and alive by keeping the jug in the icy river water. Jake could not have received better care if he had been in a hospital. He had clean white sheets on his bed, sulfa, good food, and penicillin.

In contrast, Doc, the sarge, and I were covered with fleas and lice. We tried to go down to the stream and wash—that is we tried once. They have an abundance of blow-flies in that country. A blow-fly is a little devil that, when he bites you, stings like hell and leaves an itchy, red bubble on the skin. A couple of hundred of those were a great deal worse than a few flea bites. Every time we removed our clothes to take a swim, those little things swarmed down on us in a cloud of stinging jaggers. After that I didn't wonder why the natives never washed or changed what little clothing they wore. Before we left, all the natives working for us were wearing G.I. trousers and shirts to protect their skin from the flies.

One evening the interpreter finally walked into our camp. He was wearing a red sash around his waist, over his back, and across his chest and, with an attitude to match his fancy clothes, was filled with his own self-importance. He was a Duppla who could speak both Duppla and Assamese. Of course, the only trouble was that none of us could speak either one. Who he was going to interpret for, or to, was beyond us, but he stuck around anyway and watched.

With the arrival of the dynamite and our growing expertise in its use, the runway was beginning to take on real shape, and I was beginning to believe we'd actually make a usable airstrip. We had to move Jake a couple of times while we blew the stumps near his lean-to, and we had a little trouble with the natives crowding around while we set fuses, but we managed. I didn't like the native's curiosity much; if anything happened to any of them, the others would probably take out their wrath on Doc and Jake.

Once, as we were trying to chase them away, one of them became angry and pulled a knife on Brenner. I have never seen anything move as fast as the sarge did. He could be a mean playmate when he wanted to be, and right then he wanted to be. In a flash, that native was down on the ground with the sarge on the top and his hunting knife was held, blade down, on the native's throat.

"Shall I start cuttin' this bird up, Bill, or do you want to do it?"

"Take it easy, Jim. We're slightly outnumbered here."

"What the hell do I care? Look at 'im squirm," he said as he pressed down on the knife. "Try to knife me, will ya?"

"Let him go, Jim. You've scared him enough and me, too."

"Scare him?" he yelled. "I'd like to kill the bloody bastard. Get up and run, you rat. An' run like hell before I kick your teeth in."

The last I saw of that native he was still running over the hill. We had no more trouble with any of them from that time on.

Eventually the strip was as ready as it ever would be. We had filled all the holes and leveled the bumps as well as we could with knives and what rakes the natives were able to make out of wood. Jake was champing at the bit to be on his way. The doc was completely covered with insect bites and miserable as any one man can be. The time looked about ripe.

Surrounding our strip, the natives had built a village; they were here to stay and see the fun. The traffic had been so heavy over the river that they had even built a suspension bridge of vines and bamboo. Even they were becoming anxious for the day to arrive. So the next time Bill Davis flew over, I told him any time he was ready, we were. After a couple of passes over the field he agreed the strip looked as ready as it ever would be. An L-5 liaison plane would be on the field in the morning if the weather permitted.

Our strip was 850 feet long, enough room for that type of plane. A two-seater, it was small and light and didn't need a long runway to land or take off. But taking off would be harder than landing. Getting off the ground wasn't all it had to do; the plane had to climb enough to get over the trees. To help, we cleared a path through the forest of trees at both ends of the strip. The field was bumpy, but it was as good as it ever would be, as good as we could make it. From here on out, it was completely up to the pilot.

We slept little that night. Rolled up in our parachutes in front of the fire, Brenner, Jake, Doc, and I talked late into the night. The responsibility was great, and it was all ours. If we said we didn't think a landing practical, no landing would be made; we knew that. When we had put the O.K. on it, from there on in we were the responsible parties, and if anyone was killed it was definitely our fault.

In the morning, the weather was clear as far as we could see. I was almost sorry since delay seemed like a blessing at this point; we'd done our best, but I was worried it wouldn't be good enough. The doc, though, was optimistic and had Jake all ready for the trip. He was shaved and shined up like a new baby. We carried him out on his stretcher so that he, too, could see the first landing at our "airport."

Doc, in his spare time the day before, had gotten a couple of natives to put up a bamboo tower in imitation of a real airport. With a piece of parachute and some darker material, we'd made a banner and it flew proudly in the breeze: *A.T.C.—T.D., AIR TRANSPORT COMMAND, TIBETAN DIVISION.* For a windsock, we hung up an old pair of white underdrawers with a little mustard in the right spots as an imitation of the way the pilot would feel making a landing in this hole in the mountains.

The plane flew into view and circled high above the ridges. After it came others: a couple of B-25s, our Doug with Bill Davis aboard, and another liaison plane. It looked like an aerial invasion. Bill told us over the radio that some combat cameramen had come along to take pictures, and some Army brass were aboard the Doug to see our airstrip for themselves. We set off a smoke bomb so the pilot of the tiny plane could see the wind direction on the ground, and then we waited.

He circled awhile, and we sweated him out. Maybe he wouldn't try it. Maybe the field looked too small from the air. A lot of maybes entered my mind, but I said nothing, and neither did the rest of the crowd. We were all worried, except the natives, all five hundred of them. They were all over the place, full of curiosity; they'd never seen so many planes before. Willy Watt in one of the B-25s came down and buzzed the airstrip. It was a beautiful piece of flying, and he wasn't more than six feet off the ground the entire length of the runway. The thunder of the engines was murderous.

After several slow passes over the field the little plane sailed behind a mountain, appeared again scraping the top of the saddle, and leveled off lined up with the runway. For better or worse, he was coming in.

He was a darn good pilot, setting that plane down on the first inch of runway, and with his brakes got it completely stopped before he was halfway down the strip. The plane bounced crazily over the bumps, but he kept her right. Now he turned and taxied over to us. He had made half of the job in a blaze of success, but taking off would be another matter. Could he pick up enough speed with the two of them aboard on that rough field to pull off at the end of the runway? If he couldn't, it was into the roaring river—not a pretty thought at seventy miles an hour.

Staff Sergeant William Nelson cut his engine and crawled out. His plane had the word "Arkansas" painted on the nose, so I took it for granted he was from there. I still don't know for sure, though, for we had little time for the niceties of polite society.

With everybody helping, we loaded Jake aboard. It was an ambulance ship, and the stretcher fit in the back. The natives crowded around the plane to see what made this curious bird fly. Overhead the numerous planes droned in a circle, waiting. Then we all waited as the plane taxied up to the end of the runway and started testing its engine. The natives lined both sides of the strip, and as the plane started slowly forward we held our breath.

The little plane bounced over the bumps past where we stood. It was gathering speed so slowly, and I could feel myself trying, by mental effort, to lift it into the air. It was almost at the end of the runway, and the river loomed ahead. Would he never pull back on that stick? Slowly, very slowly, it wobbled off the ground and flew down our alleyway cut in the forest. Slowly it climbed, and finally it was safe above the trees and rose over the high ridge in its path. Jake was on his way home.

Then the other little plane came in and landed. It was Dock Hudson, and were we glad to see him! "Hi, men," he called out after cutting his engine. "How are the hillbillies doin'?"

We shook hands and patted each other on the back; this was a good day. "I brought you guys a present," he said as he reached into the back of his plane. "I thought you might want to do a little celebrating if this thing went off O.K." He handed the sarge a bottle of bourbon, and he also had one for me.

Immediately Brenner opened his. "This is what I need, wow! After that takeoff, wow!" After he had a drink, he handed it to Dock, "Here, you have one and thanks for the present."

"Nope," said Dock. "Thanks anyway, but I gotta fly one of you guys back today. Which will it be?"

Jim and I elected Doc Lamberts, much over his protests.

"If Dock can get you off," I told him, "then the sarge and I will try it, but you gotta be the guinea pig."

"Fine bunch of buddies I have," grumbled the doc. "But what the hell, let's go."

They climbed aboard, and Dock Hudson taxied to the end of the runway. He tested his engine, and then he, too, started that slow, breathtaking, bumpy trip down the field. When he reached the end of the strip, he didn't have the speed the other plane had, and he shot off the end of the dirt, dipped low, his wheels skimming the water. He pulled her up into a slow climb and cleared the trees by inches.

The sensation of helplessness as we watched that plane come so near to cracking up with our two friends aboard was terrible. After we knew she was safe, the tough old sarge turned away. I knew he felt as I did about the whole thing. A lump as big as an apple was in my throat pushing tears into my eyes. Neither of us would look at the other, and speaking was out of the question at the moment. We'd come so close to losing two of our best friends, but now they were safe. We had been only kidding Doc about his going as an experiment, for after the first plane we'd felt certain the field was safe. Our joke had very nearly boomeranged on us.

We knew that no pilot would come into this field again for two men who were perfectly capable of walking out. It would have been great to ride back, but it looked like walking was the way for us. It wasn't fair to ask another pilot to risk his life unnecessarily.

22

The place seemed mighty lonely with those two birds gone, and we decided to leave as soon as we could and made arrangements with the chief to start the long trek back in the morning. We had nothing to do after that but lay around in the sun for the remainder of the day. In the late afternoon, the sarge and I went down the stream to a large pool we had seen. Hastily we pulled off our clothing and dived into the icy water. It had to be hasty, for those damn flies were hovering around looking for fresh meat. The water was so cold we were numb in a matter of minutes, but it felt wonderful.

After we had removed most of our fleas, we hoped, we put on our clothing and picked up some dynamite we had brought along. We could see two- and three-foot fish swimming around in that pool, and we were after them. We took a pound of dynamite and with a short fuse tossed it into the center of the pool. A geyser of white water shot into the air.

"That ought to do it," Jim said.

But not a fish floated to the surface. We couldn't see the fish in the pool anymore, but we tried a couple of more charges, each time larger until the last one was a two-pound load. That one nearly emptied the pool for a minute, but still no fish. We gave up.

"Nuts!" said Brenner. "Them fish saw it comin' and ducked."

"Must be. Guess we don't have fresh fish for dinner tonight."

"What's that contraption down there where those natives are?" he asked, pointing down the stream.

"Don't know. Let's go and take a look."

We walked downstream to where a group of natives was standing around a peculiar-looking arrangement of bamboo along one side of the stream. Across the stream they had built a low dam that made most of the water flow through their contraption. It looked like a boardwalk running parallel to the stream at a slight upward angle. The water poured into the mouth of it, shot up the bamboo trough, and then finally dissipated through the bamboo. It left behind, on the trough floor, anything it might have carried with it on its forward rush. The trough was full of fish, all dead.

The natives were picking them out gleefully. The fish weren't flopping about, so we knew the dynamite had killed them, then they had floated underwater, downstream, and into this trough. The sarge and I pulled out a few big ones for dinner, and we left the natives gleefully chattering over their day's catch.

Tonight they would eat fish and rice, all provided by the Americans.

The two of us sat around our campfire that night, but we didn't feel like celebrating. We had a couple of hundred miles to walk. From the wreck, Jim had brought back five big sacks full of mail, and we had to see that they were carried out, too. It was going to be quite a job.

While we sat there having a short drink from one of the celebration bottles, the chief came up and handed me some paper. He made signs that he had gotten it from one of the natives. I held the stuff down near the fire and took a look.

I gave a gasp. "Would you look at this, Jim."

"My God, we're in the chips," he said, seeing that in my hand the chief had placed a stack of American fifty dollar bills and a stack of one hundred denomination Indian notes. It totaled around two thousand bucks. I called the chief over and found out that the natives had been to the wreck, and this was just some peculiar-looking paper they had found, so they had brought it to me. Naturally it had to be turned in to the government, but it did seem unusual walking around in the jungle, where a buck was worth exactly nothing, with two thousand of them in my pocket.

"Yeah," Brenner said, "and if you was in New York where you could spend it, you'd soon be broke. Ain't life hell?"

The next morning we started back over the same trail we'd arrived on, accompanied by the usual team of native porters, including the chief and Sin Low. Unable to carry everything that had been dropped, and also because the natives had earned them, we left behind all the tools, parachutes, and equipment we'd used to build the strip.

Days and days passed as we made our agonizing way up the mountains. We were and we weren't in a hurry; in the mornings we hurried, but late in the day when the blisters grew raw and the muscles ached, we loafed.

At every village we came to, we stopped while Brenner and I set up a first aid station. In one village when we arrived, a woman was in labor. It was her first child. She didn't look much more than a child herself. I guessed her age at thirteen. The young father was frantic in his joy at seeing the American "doctor" arrive. The sarge and I went into the hut. She lay there, moaning, her knees pulled up to her stomach. When she saw us, she gave a scream of terror.

"Holy catfish," Brenner exclaimed, "don't tell me we're goin' to deliver a baby—that's the end!"

"Come on," I told him, "get some hot water and one of our towels. I've never delivered one myself, but I think I know about what happens."

I gave the woman, much over her protests, a shot of morphine to lessen the pain a little and put cool, damp cloths on her forehead. The sarge and I took off her dirty clothing and washed her filthy body as she lay on the floor. We laid down one of Jake's old sheets on top of a blanket and rolled her over on that. She lay there moaning and groaning and writhing about.

"I hope we don't have to cut 'er open to get that kid,"

Brenner said. "With only a razor blade or a hunting knife, that's gonna' be messy."

"No, she looks like she's doing O.K., I think."

The father stood back and watched us as we sweated her out. He seemed quite content to let us do as we wished. He was only a boy himself, and I guess it was his first encounter with this sort of thing. He wasn't alone in that.

I began to count her labor pains, calling them out, while Brenner kept the score on the wall with knife cuts. When they began to come quickly and things were getting hot, Brenner cleared the shack of people, even the father, and we waited. I had to help the thing along a little, and the woman's pain must have been terrific, but, with Jim holding her and the kicking she was doing, we had little trouble with the delivery.

I had heard that you held newborn babies by their feet and patted them on the fanny to make them breathe, but this little devil was so slippery I almost dropped her, but she did begin to breathe and let out a squawk. I told Jim to clean her up a little, and I attended to the mother. Sulfa and bandages were applied and we gave her a drink of bourbon. She sputtered over that, but soon fell asleep. We cleaned the baby with olive oil and wrapped it in a clean white parachute panel. Then I called the father in to look it over. We hadn't yet cleaned up the blood that was all over us, and with his wife asleep at first he thought we had killed her. When we assured him we hadn't, he walked out of the shack on a cloud.

After we cleaned the place a little to keep away the flies that were collecting, we went outside. The entire village had gathered. The baby's father handed me a live chicken and a half dozen eggs. We took them and thanked him. We pointed to the chief and said, "Name, Chief." We pointed to Sing Low and said, "Name, Sing Low." We pointed out the remainder whose names we knew, repeating their names each time. Then I pointed at the shack where the baby was and said, "Name, Peggy." The chief got the idea and after a little conversation, he also pointed to the shack, made motions as if he was nursing a baby and said, "Name, Peggy." Everyone nodded; it was agreed. I had named a Duppla baby after my wife. Some day, I thought with a grin, some explorer would come through here thinking he was in virgin territory, and what a shock he'd have when he found a girl named Peggy!

We continued on our way. We stopped a day at a river and swam and fished and rested in the sun. Out here away from any native village, there were no flies, and we were too high for mosquitoes. The days were warm and the nights cool. We had a couple of shots of bourbon in the evening before dinner. During the day we killed a deer or a few rabbits or a few squirrels or something so we always had fresh meat for food. Here, too, the natives dug up various jungle vegetables for all of us to eat. And once, Bill Davis found us and dropped us what we needed, so we didn't lack for anything important, including bourbon. All in all, it was a nice, peaceful journey.

Still, it became a little discouraging to climb a tall mountain and, when arriving at the top, look out ahead and see nothing but ranges of mountains in the distance. But eventually we crawled our way over the last range and ahead of us was the beginning of the broad valley of Assam—and almost directly below us was Mr. and Mrs. Munroe's tea plantation.

We hiked our way down, arriving late in the afternoon. They took us under their wing in grand style. We were pretty horrible-looking messes. Our hair was down our backs like a woman's, and my beard was three inches long. Mrs. Munroe was the first non-native woman we had seen in eight months, and we found ourselves so shy we could hardly talk to her without blushing. They were a grand couple. We gave the chief and his men everything they wanted, even the red blanket. Mr. Munroe gave them rice and salt and sugar, and I gave each of them a fistful of silver rupees. They in turn stripped themselves of their knives and hats and armor, giving us anything we wanted as souvenirs.

The Munroes took us into their bungalow, as they called it, but it didn't look too much like a bungalow to me. It had modernistic furniture, indirect lighting, and a bar. My trousers, however, had a huge rip in the back. I tried to keep facing Mrs. Munroe and was successful until their young daughter came in and exclaimed in surprise, "Look, Mommy, that funny-looking man has a hole in his pants." I could have crawled under the rug.

Mrs. Munroe handled the situation handily, though. "That's all right, dear. It's the new style this year in England."

They all laughed, thank heavens.

Mr. Munroe mixed up a couple of drinks for us all and ordered the servants to prepare our baths. He saw that we had clean clothes and a hot bath and a shave. It all was definitely out of this world.

That night at dinner, Brenner and I had a difficult time not cussing between every other word and not eating with our fingers. The glass-topped table and the blue napkins made our mouths open in awe. It had been a year since we'd used a napkin. The Munroes got quite a kick out of our oohing and aahing at everything we saw. Even the clean little dog that wasn't being used as a scavenger was great to have around. It had been so long since we had seen a dog like that, we had almost forgotten they existed. I played ball with the little daughter and became very homesick for my own. After the child went to bed, we sat around and talked and drank scotch from England. They also told us what they knew about the progress of the war, and it sounded pretty good, especially in Germany where the Allies were advancing fifty miles a day. A lot had happened in the weeks we'd been in the mountains.

Mr. Munroe had an airstrip on his estate that a Doug could land on. Jake had been brought here and the Doc, too. From here they were flown in the larger ship back to the base. He said a plane from our outfit had been in every couple of days to see if we were back yet. I, personally, hoped they never came. This was the ideal place to sweat out the war.

That night the sarge and I had our own room and we slept in beds with springs in them. I had no trouble sleeping, but in the morning the servant who brought us tea had quite a shock when he found Brenner rolled up in a blanket on the floor. Naturally the plane showed up that day, it was just our luck; but it was great to see Bill Davis again and Jack Knight. It was a grand reunion. We thanked the Munroes and we were off again to our own base.

Mail from home after all this time had really piled up. As before, we sat around and read with the fellows dropping into the tent to say hello.

We hadn't even had a drink, when Major Hedrick came in and said in his brusque voice, "Nice work. You did a good job. Be ready in the morning to go again; Captain Green just cracked up in Burma."

AFTERWORD

It's difficult to know why Lieutenant Diebold ended his story where he did. His rescue operations weren't finished—at least not quite yet. The Captain Green whose crash he mentions on the last page of his manuscript was James L. Green, who, while searching for a C-46 transport that had gone down over the Hump because of heavy icing, had engine trouble himself. Unable to make it back to his base, Green had gone down somewhere in the jungle. Since his plane didn't have a radio, he'd not been able to report his position. The date was March 20, 1945.

When Captain Green's single-engine PT-19 was reported overdue, a C-47 was sent out. After a thorough and unsuccessful search, the crew returned to base. As they approached for a landing they spotted the wreckage practically in the traffic pattern of their airfield, but some miles distant. The next morning, Lieutenant Diebold led a team to rescue Green, as well as the Naga chief who had been persuaded to fly with Green to help him find the missing C-46.

As it turned out, the crew of the C-46 Captain Green had been searching for was found by another search party, and together they were able to walk out of the jungle. Green, however, was badly injured, and the Naga chief had died in the crash.

Diebold, together with Doc Lamberts, eventually arranged a helicopter rescue—one of only a few conducted in the CBI theater—an evacuation that involved hacking out a landing pad in the jungle for the two-seater, YR-4 Sikorsky.

It's impossible to be sure, but that may have been Lieutenant Diebold's last major rescue; there seems to be no other record of his continuing activity. What I did find, however, was news of his own air crash, an accident that almost certainly ended his service with the 1352nd rescue unit.

On May 17, 1945, an Army newspaper, the *Hump Express*, carried the following story:

The life of 1st Lt. William Diebold, jungle rescue expert who bails out over rugged Himalaya country to aid downed and injured airmen, was saved this week by the pilot of his tiny liaison plane which crashed.

1st Lt. T. M. "Bud" Lanahan, the pilot, badly injured himself, got out of the smashed airplane. When he saw Diebold, stunned and with a broken leg, sitting in the flaming wreckage, he dashed back into the fuselage, unhooked the helpless man's safety belt and dragged Diebold to safety.

Fortunately for Diebold and Lanahan, the L-5 liaison plane crashed virtually on top of a spur to the Ledo Road and close to an Army air base. A nearby engineering unit picked them up, and within an hour both were in an Army hospital. The article—together with an interview Diebold gave to the *Pittsburgh Press* on September 23, 1945—went on to say that he had been in the plane directing a ground party to a crash site, playing the role that had often been played for him by pilots Bill Davis and Jack Knight. But it gave no other details.

That plane crash and the broken leg that came with it must have ended Diebold's career as parachutist and jungle trekker. His service with the 1352nd spanned some nine months, from late August or early September 1944 (since he didn't give a date for his arrival, it has to be guessed from the date of Lieutenant Collins's jump into the jungle) to a few days before May 17, the date of the *Hump Express* article.

It is tempting to suppose there may have been more to Lieutenant Diebold's time in the CBI than he chose to recount in *Hell Is So Green*. He seemed to inspire tales and rumors about his adventures. In *Flying the Hump*, Don Downie, for a time one of Diebold's basha-mates, tells of a raft journey that doesn't seem to be the same one Diebold tells. As Downie reports having heard, Diebold was paddling alone down a river when a cobra dropped into his raft from the trees overhead. Diebold jumped into the water, swam under the raft, and came up on the other side only to find himself face to face with the cobra. He tried the other side of the raft, and it happened again. That little game went on for quite a while before the lieutenant was finally able to get the snake off the raft and climb back in.

In another story, Diebold reportedly lost a member of one of his search parties while on a trail through the jungle when a krait, a deadly snake, struck the third man in the line, killing him in minutes. Diebold, at the head of the line, had just missed being struck himself.

But Downie ends those tales by saying: "At least that was what was reported." One has to suppose—since Diebold mentioned neither of those incidents—that they were basha scuttlebutt, tales of derring-do inspired by a man becoming something of a legend among the pilots who flew the Hump.

Whatever their origin, Diebold's story needed no such embellishments. It stands on its own. Finding himself in a certain place at a time when he could help, he did just that, leaping into surely the greatest adventure of his life.

What happened to him after the war is a bit vague, but he didn't fare well. He apparently had trouble adjusting to civilian life. Two marriages ended in divorce, he had a hard time keeping a job, and drinking affected his health—not surprising considering his and Sergeant Brenner's enthusiasm for the "medicinal" liquor that dropped so frequently from the skies. Diebold died early, in 1965, at age forty-seven.

It's harder to find out about his life after the war than about his service, but his tough time was a result, in part at least, of his experiences in the jungles of Burma—what he did, what he saw, and this great and central moment in his life. Veterans—after undergoing life-changing challenges and adventures that civilian life could hardly be expected to match—have trouble adjusting. Over the years, we have found that war produces other casualties, other injuries, than physical wounds. Fortunately for us, however, Diebold's story survived, and it is for what he did there that he is best remembered and best honored.

ACKNOWLEDGMENTS

The publication of my father's book, *Hell Is So Green*, has been a long time coming. Written shortly after the war, it languished in attics and boxes for more than sixty years. Now, thanks to the believers, his story is finally seeing the light.

Several friends, over the years, encouraged me to have my father's account of his time in Burma published. I am grateful for the loving support of my sisters, Lonna Higgins and Michele Trombley, and my cousin John Steitz, who did valuable research to substantiate the chronology of dates and events. However, the book clearly required some editing and needed someone with a special talent for approaching the material with a sensitive hand for the personal side of war. A number of people were excited and moved by my father's tale, though no one had the skills or the time to undertake the task.

I shared the manuscript with a friend, Dick Matthews, and found the perfect match between book and editor.

Dick liked it immediately. He felt passionately excited in reading the heroic adventures of my father. Dick asked if I would be willing to let him take it in hand, do some research and rewriting, and seek a publisher. I agreed. The result is the book within these pages.

Although friends had felt the book's potential, Dick saw in it a unique story of adventure and courage, understanding better than anyone had before what it would take to get it into print. For his dedication to that task, and for all the work he did, I am grateful. I thank him, above all, for recognizing that my faith in my father was not misplaced and that my father was the genuine hero I have always believed him to be.

—Penelope Diebold

It has been fascinating research and an absorbing task. They were brave days and brave men who served there. I feel as if I've gotten to know some of the people in Diebold's book, and I find I like them. Especially I've come to like Bill Diebold.

To my wife, Pam, a special thanks for her invaluable help and patience in letting me run with this.

And to Penelope, thank you for trusting me with this piece of your father's life. And to all of Bill's family, who lost him much too early, may this story awaken him again in your hearts.

—Richard Matthews